The Migration Conference 2025 Programme

THE MIGRATION CONFERENCE

UNIVERSITY OF GREENWICH

LATITUDE 51°28'28" NORTH
LONGITUDE 0°00'00"

I0116131

EAST   WEST

11-17 JUNE   LONDON
2025

UNIVERSITY OF GREENWICH

TRANSNATIONAL PRESS® LONDON

INTERNATIONAL BUSINESS SCHOOL

Greenwich Campus

London SE10 9LS

UNIVERSITY OF GREENWICH

Maze Hill — 8 mins walk in Tom Smith Close.

13. Hamilton House approximately 400m from Greenwich Campus.

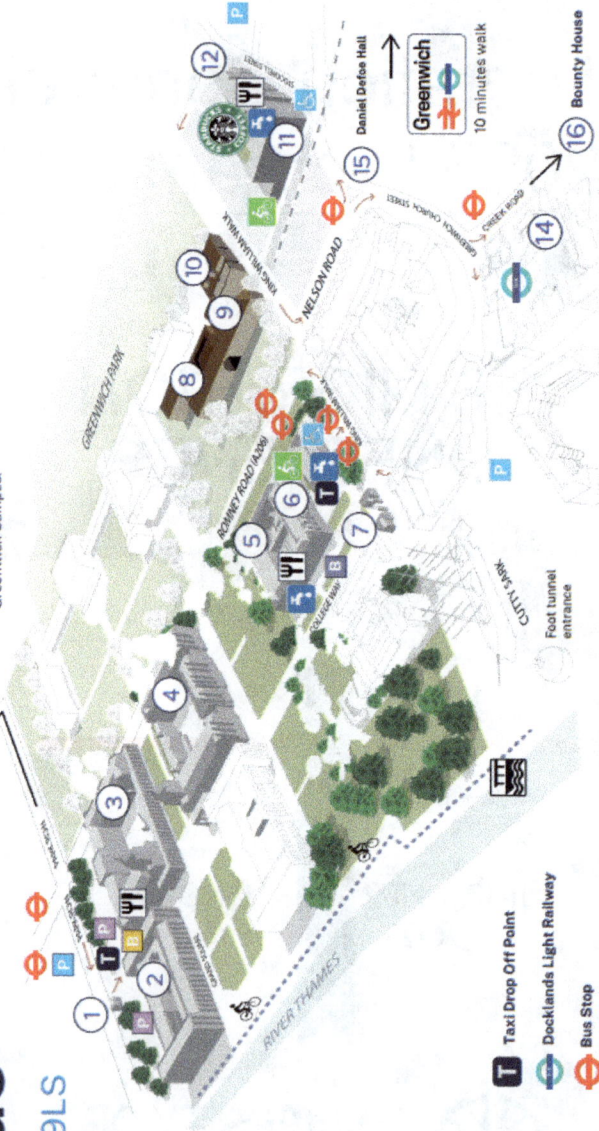

Greenwich — 10 minutes walk

Daniel Defoe Hall

Landmarks / labels on map: GREENWICH PARK, VINCENT WILLIAM WALK, NELSON ROAD, ROMNEY ROAD/A206, COLLEGE WAY, KING WILLIAM WALK, GREENWICH CHURCH STREET, CREEK ROAD/A200, CUTTY SARK, RIVER THAMES, Foot tunnel entrance

1. East Gate Entrance
2. Queen Anne Court
3. Queen Mary Court
4. King William Court
5. Dreadnought
6. Stephen Lawrence Building
7. West Gate Entrance
8. Devonport House
   Academic
9. Devonport House
   Halls of residence
10. Cooper Powerhouse
    London SE10 9JH
11. Stockwell Street
    Library
12. Stockwell Street
    Academic
13. Hamilton House
    15 Park Vista, SE10 9LZ
14. Cutty Sark Hall
    London SE10 9ED
15. Daniel Defoe Hall
    London SE10 9FY
16. Bounty House
    London SE8 3DE
    International college

Legend:
- Taxi Drop Off Point
- Docklands Light Railway
- Bus Stop
- University Bus Stop (to Medway)
- University Bus Stop (to Avery Hill)
- Public Parking
- Permit holders only
- Disabled Parking
- Bike compound
- Restaurant/Café
- Riverboat Services
- Water fountains

Venues: King William Court: KW002, KW003, KW016, KW302, KW303, KW315; **Queen Mary Court:** QM068, QM069 and **National Maritime Museum**

The Migration Conference 2025 Programme

compiled by
The Migration Conference Team

TRANSNATIONAL PRESS LONDON
2025

Conference Series: 35
The Migration Conference 2025 Programme
Compiled by The Migration Conference Team

Copyright © 2025 by Transnational Press London

All rights reserved.

First Published in 2025 by Transnational Press London in the United
Kingdom, 21 Woodville Drive, Sale, M33 6NF, UK.
www.tplondon.com

Transnational Press London® and the logo and its affiliated brands are
registered trademarks.
This publication or any portion thereof may not be reproduced or used in
any manner whatsoever without the express written permission of the
publisher except for the use of brief quotations in a book review or
scholarly journal.
Requests for permission to reproduce material from this work should be
sent to: sales@tplondon.com

ISBN:
978-1-80135-328-1 (Print)
978-1-80135-330-4 (Digital)

CONTENT & TIMETABLE
Please note [All London, UK Times]

Since the first event in 2012, the Migration Conferences have drawn thousands of attendees from around the world. These conferences have been hosted in various capital cities including Mexico City (2024), Hamburg (2023), Rabat (2022), London (2012, 2014, 2021), Tetovo/London (2020), Bari (2019), Lisbon (2018), Athens (2017), Vienna (2016), Prague (2015). The 13th Migration Conference is hosted by the University of Greenwich, London, UK. This event serves as a global forum for academics, policymakers, practitioners, students, and others interested in engaging in meaningful debate and research-driven discussions on the impacts of human mobility worldwide.

Sponsors and Supporters of The Migration Conferences – past and present:

Universities

University of Greenwich, London, UK (TMC 2025 Host)
International Business School (IBS), Manchester, UK (2021-2025)
Universidad Iberoamericana, Mexico City, Mexico (TMC 2024 Host)
Universität Hamburg, Germany (TMC 2023 Host)
Albrecht Mendelssohn Bartholdy Graduate School of Law, Germany (TMC 2023 Host)
Mohammad V University, Rabat, Morocco (TMC 2022 Host)
South East European University, N. Macedonia (TMC 2020 Host)
University of Bari Aldo Moro, Italy (TMC 2019 Host)
University of Bari, Dipartimento di Scienze Politiche, Italy (TMC 2019 Host)
University of Lisbon, ISEG and IGOT, Portugal (TMC 2018 Host)
Harokopio University, Athens (TMC 2017 Host)
University of Vienna, Austria (TMC 2016 Host)
Charles University Prague Faculty of Humanities, Czech Republic (TMC 2015 Host)
Regent's University London, UK (2012-2014 Host)
CENTRUS – Centro Transdisciplinar Universitario para la sustentabilidad
Danube University Krems, Austria
El Colegio de Mexico, Mexico
Hefei University, Sino-German Economic Development and Innovation Research Centre, P.R. China
Istanbul Beykent University, Türkiye
Ruhr-Universität Bochum, Centre for Mediterranean Studies, Germany
Ruppin Academic Centre, Israel
Social Sciences University of Ankara, Global Migration Research Centre, Türkiye
Istanbul Topkapi University, Migration Policies Research Centre, Türkiye
Migration Institute, Finland
Moscow City University, Russia
Polissia National University, Ukraine
Symbiosis International University, India
The Ohio State University, The Global Mobility Project, USA
Unidad Académica en Estudios del Desarrollo, Mexico

Universidad de Burgos, Spain
Universidad Latina de México, Mexico
Universidad Tecnica Partocular de Loja, Ecuador
Universidade de Lisboa, Research Centre in Economic and Organizational Sociology (SOCIUS), Portugal (2018)
University of California Gifford Center for Population Studies
University of Notre Dame, USA
University of Nottingham, Faculty of Humanities and Social Sciences, China
West Ukrainian National University, Ternopil, Ukraine
Yaşar University Jean Monnet Migration Chair, Türkiye

Organisations and Companies
American Chamber in Mexico
CEEY – Centro de Estudios Espinosa Yglesias
Consejo Noruego para Refugiados
Patronato de la Ibero FICSAC
l'Association Marocaine d'Etudes et de Recherches sur les Migrations (AMERM), Morocco (TMC 2022 Host)
The National Human Rights Council (CNDH), Morocco (2022)
Austrian Air – Official Carrier for TMC 2016
Centre for Development Evaluation and Social Science Research (CREDI), Sarajevo, Bosnia and Herzegovina
Claussen Simon Stiftung, Germany (2023)
EKKE – The National Center of Social Research, Greece (2017)
Global Policy and Strategy, Ankara, Türkiye (2014)
Hellenic Sociological Society (2017)
Institut de Recherche, Formation et Action sur les Migrations, Belgium
IUSSP International Migration Expert Panel (2011-2015)
J. Hornig Coffee (2015)
Ming-Ai (London) Institute, United Kingdom
Hassan II Foundation for Moroccans Residing Abroad, Morocco (2022)
Refugee Law Clinic, Hamburg, Germany (2023)
Ria Money Transfers (2011-2014)
RGS Population Studies Group, United Kingdom (2011-2014)
Sustainable Equity and Social Studies Association (SEDER)
Western Balkans Migration Network (WB-MIGNET), Bosnia and Herzegovina
ZEIT Stiftung, Ebelin und Gerd Bucerius, Germany (2023)

Cities and Other Agencies
International Organisation for Migration (2011-2014, 2024)
National Maritime Museum, Greenwich, UK
National Office of Social and Cultural University Works, Morocco (2022)
The Ministry of Education, Morocco (2022)
ISTAT (Italian National Statistics Office) (2019)
Municipality of Bari, Italy (2019)

United Nations Population Fund (UNFPA)
Ordine Assistenti Sociali Regione Puglia, Italy (2019)
Puglia Regional Administration, Italy (2019)
Red Cross, Italy (2019)
Tourism Office of Lisbon, Portugal (2018)
Vienna Convention Bureau, Austria (2016)

Promoting Journals and Publishers
Yeiya
International Journal of Human Mobility
Migration and Diversity
Göç Dergisi
Border Crossing
Transnational Education Review
Transnational Press London, UK

migrationconference.net
fb.me/MigrationConference
    Email: migrationscholar@gmail.com

Host Institutions of The Migration Conferences

- University of Greenwich, UK (TMC 2025 Host)
- Universidade Iberoamericana, Mexico (TMC 2024 Host)
- Universität Hamburg, Germany (TMC 2023 Host)
- Mohammed V University of Rabat, Morocco (TMC 2022 Host)
- Association Marocaine d'Etudes & de Recherches sur les Migrations (AMERM), Morocco (TMC 2022 Host)
- International Business School, UK (TMC 2021 Host)
- Ming-Ai (London) Institute, UK (TMC 2021 Host)
- South East European University, N. Macedonia (TMC 2020 Host)
- University of Bari Aldo Moro, Italy (TMC 2019 Host)
- University of Bari, Italy (TMC 2019 Host)
- Universidade de Lisboa, Portugal (TMC 2018 Host)
- Harokopio University, Athens, Greece (TMC 2017 Host)
- University of Vienna, Austria (TMC 2016 Host)
- Charles University Prague, Czech Republic (TMC 2015 Host)
- Regent's University London, UK (TMC 2014 Host)
- Regent's College London, UK (TMiE 2012 Host)

People

The Migration Conference Executive Team

Prof Ibrahim Sirkeci, International Business School, Manchester, UK (Chair)
Prof Özgür H. Çınar, University of Greenwich, UK (Chair)
Prof Jeffrey H. Cohen, Ohio State University, USA
Prof Philip L Martin, University of California Davis, USA
Dr Ülkü Sezgi Sözen, University of Hamburg, Germany
Dr Karla Angélica Valenzuela-Moreno, Universidad Iberoamericana, Mexico

Transnational Advisory Committee

Prof Gudrun Biffl, Krems, Austria
Professor Özgür H. Çınar, University of Greenwich, UK
Prof Lucinda Fonseca, University of Lisbon, Portugal
Prof Elli Heikkila, Migration Institute of Finland, Finland
Prof Mohamed Khachani, Mohammed V University of Rabat, Morocco
Prof Beatrice Knerr, Kassell University, Germany and Hefei University, China
Prof Markus Kotzur, University of Hamburg, Germany
Prof Jonathan Liu, International Business School, UK
Prof Apostolos G Papadopoulos, Harokopio University of Athens, Greece
Prof Carla Pederzini, Universidad Iberoamericana, Mexico
Prof João Peixoto, University of Lisbon, Portugal
Prof Michela C. Pellicani, University of Bari "Aldo Moro", Italy
Prof Giuseppe Sciortino, University of Trento, Italy
Dr Karla Angélica Valenzuela-Moreno, Universidad Iberoamericana, Mexico

Scientific Review Committee
Africa

Agnes Igoye, Ministry of Interior Affairs, Uganda
Prof Mohamed Khachani, AMERM & Mohammed V University of Rabat, Morocco
Dr Rania Rafik Khalil, The British University in Egypt, Egypt
Dr Sadhana Manik, University of KwaZulu-Natal, South Africa
Prof Claude Sumata, National Pedagogical University, DR Congo
Dr Ayman Zohry, Egyptian Society for Migration Studies, Egypt

Americas

Prof Jeffrey H. Cohen, Ohio State University, USA
Dr José Salvador Cueto-Calderón, Universidad Autónoma de Sinaloa, Mexico
Dr Ana Vila Freyer, Universidad de Guanajuato, Mexico
Dr Pascual G. García-Macías, Universidad Técnica Particular de Loja, Ecuador

Dr Carlos Alberto González Zepeda, Universidad Autónoma Metropolitana-Cuajimalpa, Mexico
Dr Torunn Haaland, Gonzaga University, USA
Prof Liliana Jubilut, Universidade Católica de Santos, Brazil
Prof Philip L Martin, University of California Davis, USA
Prof Carla Pederzini, Universidad Iberoamericana, Mexico
Dr Eric M. Trinka, Emory & Henry College, USA
Karla Angélica Valenzuela-Moreno, Universidad Iberoamericana, Mexico
Dr Hassan Vatanparast, Saskatchewan University, Canada
Prof Rodolfo García Zamora, Autonomous University of Zacatecas, Mexico
Dr Monette Zard, Columbia University, USA

Asia-Pacific

Prof Ram Bhagat, International Institute for Population Sciences, India
Dr Jocelyn O. Celero, University of the Philippines Diliman, Philippines
Dr Sadaf Mahmood, University of Agriculture Faisalabad, Pakistan
Dr Shweta Sinha Deshpande, Symbiosis School for Liberal Arts, India
Prof Nicholas Procter, University of South Australia, Australia
Dr Ruchi Singh, Indian Institute of Management, Bengaluru, India
Dr AKM Ahsan Ullah, University Brunei Darussalam, Brunei
Dr Xi Zhao, Hefei University, P.R. China

Central and Eastern Europe

Dr Merita Zulfiu Alili, South East European University, N. Macedonia
Dr Olga R. Gulina, Benefit Research GMBH, Germany
Dr Nermin Oruc, Centre for Development Evaluation and Social Science Research (CREDI), Sarajevo, Bosnia and Herzegovina
Prof Apostolos G Papadopoulos, Harokopio University of Athens, Greece
Prof Irina Savchenko, Moscow City University, Russian Federation

Western Europe

Prof Bahar Baser, Durham University, United Kingdom
Prof Aron Anselem Cohen, University of Granada, Spain
Dr Martina Cvajner, University of Trento, Italy
Dr Carla de Tona, University of Bologna, Italy
Dr Sureya Sonmez Efe, University of Lincoln, United Kingdom
Dr Alina Esteves, Universidade de Lisboa, Portugal
Dr Setenay Dilek Fidler, University of Westminster, United Kingdom
Prof Monica Ibáñez-Angulo, University of Burgos, Spain
Dr Gul Ince Beqo, University of Urbino, Italy
Prof Jonathan Liu, International Business School, United Kingdom
Dr Lan Lo, University of Nottingham, United Kingdom

Dr Altay Manço, IRFAM, Belgium
Dr A. Erdi Öztürk, London Metropolitan University, United Kingdom
Dr Andrea Romano, Faculty of Law, University of Barcelona, Spain
Dr Sahizer Samuk-Carignani, University of Pisa, Italy
Prof Mario Savino, University of Tuscia, Italy
Prof Giuseppe Sciortino, University of Trento, Italy
Dr Caner Tekin, Ruhr-Universität Bochum, Germany
Dr Irene Tuzi, Sapienza University of Rome, Italy
Dr Ülkü Sezgi Sözen, University of Hamburg, Germany

Near East

Prof Sebnem Koser Akcapar, Ankara Social Sciences University, Türkiye
Dr Deniz Yetkin Aker, Istanbul Beykent University, Türkiye
Dr Tuncay Bilecen, Kocaeli University, Türkiye
Prof Dilek Cindoglu, Yasar University, Türkiye
Prof Yaprak Civelek, Anadolu University, Türkiye
Dr Z. Banu Dalaman, SEDER, Türkiye
Prof Sevim Atilla Demir, Sakarya University, Türkiye
Dr İnci Aksu Kargın, Uşak University, Türkiye
Prof Yakhnich Liat, Beit Berl College, Israel
Dr Armagan Teke Lloyd, Abdullah Gul University, Türkiye
Prof Gökay Özerim, Yaşar University, Türkiye
Dr Md Mizanur Rahman, Qatar University, Qatar
Dr Betul Dilara Seker, Van Yuzuncu Yil University, Türkiye
Dr Paulette K. Schuster, Reichman University, Israel
Dr Onur Unutulmaz, Ankara Social Sciences University, Türkiye
Dr Deniz Eroglu Utku, Trakya University, Türkiye
Dr Nevin Karabiyik Yerden, Marmara University, Türkiye
Dr Pınar Yazgan, Sakarya University, Türkiye

The Migration Conference Technical Organisation Committee

Dr Aytac Yerden, Gedik University, Türkiye (IT)
Ege Cakir, Middle East Technical University, Türkiye (Admin)

The Migration Conferences team are proud to have leading scholars and experts in the field as keynote speakers and panellists. This year, TMC will feature:

- Ozlem **Onaran**, University of Greenwich, UK
- Bill **Bowring**, Birkbeck College, University of London, UK
- Jeffrey H. **Cohen**, Ohio State University, USA
- Philip L. **Martin**, University of California, Davis, USA
- Mario **Savino**, University of Tuscia, Italy

In previous years, The Migration Conferences entertained distinguished scholars delivering keynote speeches including:
Fiona B. Adamson, SOAS, University of London, UK [2019], Theresa Alfaro-Velcamp, Emeritus Professor, Sonoma State University, USA [2021], Joaquin Arango, Complutense University of Madrid, Spain [2018], Jürgen Bast, Justus-Liebig-Universität Gießen, Germany [2023], Giuseppe Brescia, MP, Member of Italian Chamber of Deputies, Parliamento Italiano, Italy [2020], Caroline Brettell, Southern Methodist University, USA [2015], Gabriele Buchholtz, University of Hamburg, Germany [2023], Pedro Calado, The High Commissioner for Migration, Lisbon, Portugal [2018], Barry Chiswick, George Washington University, USA [2014], Prof Jeffrey H. Cohen, Ohio State University, United States [2022], Martina Cvajner, University of Trento, Italy [2020], Luisa Feline Freier De Ferrari, Universidad del Pacifico, Peru [2023], Jelena Dzankic, Co-Director of the GLOBALCIT Network, European University Institute, Italy [2020], Élise Féron, Tampere Peace Research Institute, Tampere University, Finland [2021], Nissa Finney, University of St Andrews, UK [2020], Elli Heikkilä, Research Director, Migration Institute of Finland, Finland [2020], James F. Hollifield, Director of the Tower Center for Public Policy and International Affairs at Southern Methodist University, Dallas, USA [2021], Agnes Igoye, Deputy National Coordinator Prevention of Trafficking in Persons, Ministry of Internal Affairs, Uganda [2020], Markus Koller, Ruhr-Universität Bochum, Germany [2022], Michelle Leighton, International Labour Organization, Genève, Switzerland [2018], Philip L. Martin, University of California, Davis, USA [2019], Markus Kotzur, University of Hamburg, Germany [2019], Douglas S. Massey, Princeton University, USA [2015], Helén Nilsson, Director, Nordic Council of Ministers Office in Lithuania [2020], Mustafa Ozbilgin, Brunel University London, UK [2022], Karsten Paerregaard, Gothenburg University, Sweden [2019], Karen Phalet, KU Leuven, Belgium [2016], Rodolfo Cruz Piñeiro, Director, Departamento de Estudios de Población, El Colegio de la Frontera Norte, Mexico [2021], Irudaya Rajan, IIMAD, Kerala, India [2022], Pia M. Orrenius, Vice President and Senior Economist Federal Reserve Bank of Dallas, USA [2021], Martin Ruhs, European University Institute, Florence, Italy [2019], Mario Savino, University of Tuscia, Italy [2023], Oded Stark, University of Bonn,

Germany [2017], Ruba Salih, SOAS, University of London, UK [2018], Sasskia Sassen, Columbia University, USA [2017], Giuseppe Sciortino, University of Trento, Italy [2017], Carlos Vargas Silva, University of Oxford, UK [2019], Ibrahim Sirkeci, International Business School, UK [2016], Daniel Thym, Universität Konstanz, Germany [2023], Hna. Leticia Gutiérrez Valderrama, Scalabrinian Missionary, founder of SMR and Sergio Mendez Arceo National Human Rights Prize in Mexico; Diocesan Delegate for Migration - Diocese of Sigüenza-Guadalajara-Spain [2021], V.J. Varghese, University of Hyderabad, India [2022], María Dolores París Pombo, COLEF-Tijuana, Mexico [2024], Margarita Núñez, Universidad Iberoamericana, Mexico [2024], Estela Rivero, University of Notre Dame, USA [2024], Cecilia Menjívar, University of California, Los Angeles, USA [2024], Alejandro Anaya, Universidad Iberoamericana, Mexico [2024], Ingmar Weber, Saarland University, Germany [2024], Eva Dziadula, University of Notre Dame, USA [2024], Alfredo Cuecuecha, Universidad Popular Autónoma del Estado de Puebla, Mexico [2024], Laura Canche (IOM) [2024], Fabio Jimenez (IOM) [2024], Pedro Paulo Orraca (Colef) [2024], Pedro Casasalatriste (Amcham) [2024], Jorge Schiavon, Universidad Iberoamericana, Mexico [2024], Silvia Giorguli, El Colegio de México, Mexico [2024], Agustin Escobar Latapí, CIESAS Occidente, Mexico [2024], José Alberto Lara Pulido, Universidad Iberoamericana, Mexico [2024], Roman Hoffmann, International Institute for Applied Systems Analysis, Austria [2024], Fernando Ríosmena, University of Texas, San Antonio, USA [2024], Roberto Vélez, Centro de Estudios Espinosa Yglesias, Mexico [2024], Alfredo Cuecuecha, University of Notre Dame [2024], Norma Fuentes Mayorga, City University of New York, USA, Cesar Velázquez Guadarrama, Iberoamericana, Mexico [2024].

11 JUNE 2025 WEDNESDAY - DAY 1 [All London Times]

08:30-16:00 – Registration (King William Building, 3rd Floor)

09:30-10:00 – Opening Session [KW303 - King William Building, 3rd Floor] [Join via MS Teams]

- Welcoming speeches

10:00-11:15 – Distinguished Keynote – Plenary Discussion Session [KW303] [Join via MS Teams]

- Emeritus Professor Bill **Bowring**, FAcSS, Birkbeck College, University of London, UK
- Discussant: Professor Mario **Savino**, University of Tuscia, Italy

11:15 – 11:30: Break

11:30 – 13:00: Parallel Sessions: 1A – 1B – 1C – 1D – 1E – 1F

13:00 – 14:00: Lunch Break

14:00 – 15:30: Parallel Sessions: 2A – 2B – 2C – 2D – 2E – 2F

15:30 – 15:45: Break

15:45 – 17:15: Parallel Sessions: 3A – 3B – 3C – 3D – 3E – 3F

12 June 2025 THURSDAY - DAY 2

09:00 – 10:30: Parallel Sessions: 4A – 4B – 4C – 4D – 4E

09:00 – 10:30: 4F: Roundtable: "Food Security among Afghan Refugees" [Room: KW303][Join via Teams]
Chair: Hassan **Vatanparast**, University of Saskatchewan, Canada
- **Panellists:**
  - Mohammad Reza **Pakravan-Charvadeh**, Lorestan University, Iran
  - Ginny **Lane**, University of Idaho, USA
  - Rasoul **Sadeghi**, University of Tehran, Iran
  - Nasrin **Omidvar**, Shahid Beheshti University of Medical Sciences, Iran

10:30 – 10:45: Break

10:45 – 12:15: Parallel Sessions: 5A – 5B – 5C – 5D – 5E – 5F

12:15 – 13:15: Lunch Break

13:15 – 14:45: Plenary Discussion Session: "Migration Policy Changes in the New Era of Uncertainty"
> **[KW303] [Join via Teams]**
> **Keynote Speakers:**
> - Emeritus Professor Philip L. **Martin**, University of California Davis, USA
> - Professor Ozlem **Onaran**, University of Greenwich, UK
> - Discussant: Professor Jeffrey H. **Cohen**, Ohio State University, USA

14:45 – 15:00: Break

15:00 – 16:30: Parallel Sessions: 6A – 6B – 6C – 6D – 6E – 6F

16:30 – 16:45: Break

16:30 – 18:00: 7X National Maritime Museum - Migration Related Object Tour Lecture Theatre of the National Maritime Museum >>> **Free booking required: Please book via this link: https://tickets.rmg.co.uk/webstore/shop/viewItems.aspx?cg=MIOT&c=MIOTC**

16:45 – 18:15: Parallel Sessions: 7A – 7B – 7C – 7D – 7E – 7F

CONFERENCE DINNER
12 June 2025, Thursday
19:30-22:00 – **Conference Gala Dinner** at: The Old Brewery, Greenwich.
Directions: Google Map

13 June 2025 FRIDAY - DAY 3

FREE MORNING

13:00 – 14:30: Parallel Sessions: 8A – 8B – 8C – 8D – 8E

14:30 – 14:45: Break

14:45 – 16:15: Parallel Sessions: 9A – 9B – 9C – 9D

16:15 – 16:30: Break

16:30 – 18:00: Parallel Sessions: 10A – 10B – 10C – 10D

18:00 – 18:30: 11XA Drinks Reception at the National Maritime Museum [click here for free registration]

Followed by

     18:30 – 20:30: 11XB Film Screening with Artists at the National Maritime Museum, Lecture Theatre

16 June 2025 MONDAY – VIRTUAL SESSIONS [All London Times]

09:00 – 10:30: Parallel Sessions: 12A – 12B – 12C – 12D

10:30 – 11:00: Break

11:00 – 12:30: Parallel Sessions: 13A – 13B – 13C – 13D

12:30 – 13:30: Break

13:30 – 15:00: Parallel Sessions: 14A – 14B – 14C – 14D

15:00 – 15:30: Break

15:30 – 17:00: Parallel Sessions: 15A – 15B – 15C – 15D

17:00 – 17:30: Break

17:30 – 19:00: Parallel Sessions: 16A – 16B – 16C – 16D

17 June 2025 TUESDAY – VIRTUAL SESSIONS [All London Times]

09:00 – 10:30: Parallel Sessions: 17A – 17B – 17C

10:30 – 11:00: Break

11:00 – 12:30: Parallel Sessions: 18A – 18B – 18C

12:30 – 13:30: Break

13:30 – 15:00: Parallel Sessions: 19A – 19B – 19C – 19D

END OF THE PROGRAMME

Please note this programme is subject to change without notice.

11 June 2025, Wednesday
08:30 - 16:00 – REGISTRATION
[King William Building, 3rd Floor]

11 June 2025, Wednesday
09:30 – 10:00
Opening Session [KW303 – King William Building, 3rd Floor]

Join via MS Teams

Welcoming Speeches
- Professor Jane **Harrington**, Vice Chancellor and CEO, University of Greenwich, UK
- Professor Özgür H. **Çınar**, School of Law and Criminology, University of Greenwich, UK.
- Professor Ibrahim **Sirkeci**, International Business School, Manchester, UK
- Professor Radoslav **Stefancik**, Economics University in Bratislava, Slovakia

10:00-11:15
Distinguished Keynote – Plenary Discussion Session
[KW303 – King William Building, 3rd Floor]

Join via MS Teams
- Emeritus Professor Bill **Bowring**, FAcSS, Birkbeck College, University of London, UK
- Discussant: Professor Mario **Savino**, University of Tuscia, Italy

11:15 – 11:30: Break

11 June 2025, Wednesday
11:30 - 13:00
1A   Arts, Literature, Media 1   [Room: KW302]

Join via MS Teams

Moderator: Julie Ham, Brock University, Canada

790   Postmigration and Identity: A Comparative Study of British-Middle Eastern Narratives
  Elena Violaris, University of Oxford, UK

634   You Have Potential, But...
       Jay Mar Albaos, KU Leuven and LUCA School of Arts, Belgium
973   Stories from the Venezuelan Diaspora: Absurdity, Imagination and
       Hope
       Sherezade García Rangel, University of Lincoln, UK
680   Creative Writing Pedagogies for Labour Migration Diasporas
       Julie Ham, Brock University, Canada
       Yvonne Yevan Yu, Hong Kong Baptist University, Hong Kong

1B   Education and Skilled Migration 1   [Room: KW303]
Join via MS Teams
Moderator: Alicia Rusoja, University of California, Davis, USA
758   Venezuelan Im/migration & Education in the United States of
       America: A Qualitative Literature Review
       Alicia Rusoja, University of California, Davis, USA
445   Stories of ESOL in Suffolk, England
       Amna Smith, University of Southampton, UK
897   A Dream No Longer Deferred: The Power and Limits of Conditional
       Integration on the Social Mobility of Undocumented Young Adults
       Hyein Lee, CUNY Graduate Center, USA
       Maria Gabriela Pacheco, TheDream, USA
2025   Analysing the influence of health and mental well-being on African
       migrants
       Olivia Joseph-Aluko, Queen Mary's University, UK

1C   Identity and Migration 1   [Room: KW315]
Join via MS Teams
*Moderator: Sunday Israel Oyebamiji, Instituto Universitário de
Lisboa, Portugal*
769   The Legal Identity of Indigenous People and Borders: The Wayuu
       People in Colombia
       Pilar Balbuena, Carleton University, Ottawa, Ontario, Canada
808   Navigating Transnational Identity: The Experience of Older Migrants
       in South Africa
       Sunday Israel Oyebamiji, Instituto Universitário de Lisboa, Portugal
       Paul Kariuki, University of KwaZulu-Natal, South Africa
       Feyisetan Eniola Elebijo, University of KwaZulu-Natal, South Africa
512   Social media and migration: What is more of Africa and African
       migrants in South Africa?
       Toyin Cotties Adetiba, University of Zululand, South Africa

544 "Refugee Camps" in China: The Role of Overseas Chinese Farms in Integrating Refugees
Li Zeming, City University of Hong Kong, Hong Kong, China

1D   Families and Households 1   [Room: KW002]
Join via MS Teams
Moderator: Jocelyn Omandam Celero, University of the Philippines Diliman, Philippines

662   The importance of collaborative and multidisciplinary work in the co-construction of a digital healthcare support project for immigrant women in Quebec
Erika Corona Velazquez, Laval University, Canada
Marielle M'bangha, Perinatal Care Reference Service for Migrant Women from Quebec, Canada
Marie-Pierre Gagnon, Laval University, Canada

756   Living In-Between: Belonging and Second-Generation Latinx Emerging Adults
Maria Ximena Maldonado-Morales, Smith College School for Social Work, USA

546   Navigating Love, Caregiving, and Emotional Burdens: The Complexities of Transnational Fatherhood
Syed Imran Haider, Ca Foscari University of Venice, Italy
Francesco Della Puppa, Ca Foscari University of Venice, Italy

654   Fathering in International Marriage Families: Intergenerational Comparison of Fathering Practices and Negotiations of Mixedness among Japanese Migrant Me
Jocelyn Omandam Celero, University of the Philippines Diliman, Philippines

1E   Integration and Migration 1   [Room: KW003]
Join via MS Teams
Moderator: Ana Vila-Freyer, Universidad Latina de México

456   Reevaluating Immigrant Integration in "Exclusionary" Regimes: Diaspora and Mobility in the State of Qatar
Amanda Garrett, Georgetown University, Qatar

508   Tales of a Yiddish land. Exploring Yiddish diasporic territoriality in New York through autobiographical narratives
Ariel Roemer, Université Libre de Bruxelles, Belgium

429   Analyzing the Approach of the Government in Migration and Development through Diaspora Identities

Aurora Suarez Llige, University of the Philippines, Philippines

710   The Concept of Filial Piety Among Chinese Migrants in Ireland
       Liwei Zhu, Technological University Dublin, Ireland

1F   Migration and Development 1   [Room: KW016]

Join via MS Teams

Moderator: Djamila Chekrouni, Mohamed V University Rabat, Morocco

513   The Impact of International Migration on the Demographics and
       Economy of Morocco
       Zaynab Benabdallah, Mohamed V University Rabat, Morocco
       Djamila Chekrouni, Mohamed V University Rabat, Morocco

485   Impact of Migrants' Remittances and COVID-19 on Household
       Poverty and Inequality: A case Study of Mazar-i-Sharif, Balkh
       Province, Afghanistan
       Baqir Khawari, University of Tsukuba, Japan

647   Space and time variations in the migration and development debate-
       introducing the spatial temporal dialectic
       *Maria Teresa Pinto da Silva e Conceição Santos, University of
       Lisbon, Portugal*

796   Driven to Leave: Analyzing the factors behind emigration in Africa
       Enrica Di Stefano, Bank of Italy, Italy
       Elena Rossi Espagnet, University La Sapienza of Rome, Italy

13:00 – 14:00: Lunch Break

11 June 2025, Wednesday
14:00 - 15:30
2A   Arts, Literature, Media 2   [Room: KW302]

Join via MS Teams

Moderator: Jay Mar Albaos, KU Leuven and LUCA School of Arts, Belgium

824   Crossing the Border on TikTok: Documenting Irregular Journeys
       through Novel Social Media Platforms
       *Moaz Nasser Saber Abdelrahman, Scuola Normale Superiore di
       Pisa, Italy*
       Andrew Fallone, University of Cambridge, UK

506   The Migrant Crisis and Media Agendas: A Comparative Analysis in
       Europe
       Maija Ozola-Schade, Technical University Ilmenau, Germany

881   Young artists in exile: Comprehending the life trajectories and

artivism of displaced young adult artists in Paris. A case study of Paris in the mid-2020s

> *Plaifon Parama, Université Paris Cité & Learning Planet Institute, France*

2B   Education and Skilled Migration 2   [Room: KW303]

Join via MS Teams

Moderator: Réka Brigitta Szaniszló, University of Szeged, Hungary

852   The "#reverse_brain_drain" Campaign in Bangladesh: Public Opinion and Possibilities for Policy Change
> *Ishrar Habib, Bangladesh Association of Commonwealth Scholars and Fellows (BACSAF), Bangladesh*

742   International Student Migration Index - Theory and Application
> *Réka Brigitta Szaniszló, University of Szeged, Hungary*

2037   Student migration from India and changing policy regimes
> *Sadananda Sahoo, Indira Gandhi National Open University, India*

537   Artist as Citizenship: (Im)Mobility & (Non)Belonging
> *Ziyue Lu, University of Amsterdam, the Netherlands*

2C   Gender and Migration 1   [Room: KW315]

Join via MS Teams

Moderator: Carla De Tona, University of Bologna, Italy

944   Young Indian Migrant Women in Italy: Negotiating Gendered Emancipation Amidst Mobility, Patriarchy and Racism
> *Carla De Tona, University of Bologna, Italy*

610   Migration, Diversity, and Social Inequalities Among Generations of Women in Spain
> *Anna Montfort Chipell, Centro de Estudios Demográficos (CED-CERCA) y Universidad Autónoma de Barcelona, Spain*
> *Pau Miret Gamundi, Centro de Estudios Demográficos (CED-CERCA), Spain*
> *Andreu Domingo Valls, Centro de Estudios Demográficos (CED-CERCA), Spain*

723   "I'm a migrant and a mom; how did I find my tribe?". Ma.mi.lab and the migrant women's resilience in Belgium
> *Fanny Margot Tudela Poblete, CA Actores Sociales y Desarrollo Comunitario, Ma.mi.lab ASBL, Belgium*
> *Carolina del Valle Rodríguez, Ma.mi. Lab, Belgium*

914   Between Home and Horizon: Gendered Vulnerabilities, Health, and the Long Walk of Migration in India

*Munappy Gayatri Gopinathan, Cochin University of Science and
Technology, India*
P R Suresh, Cochin University of Science and Technology, India

2D   Integration and Migration 2   [Room: KW002]
Join via MS Teams
Moderator: Yael Gordon, LSE, UK

434   Securitizing Rohingyas: exploring exclusionary dynamics in India's
        security discourse
        Monika Verma, Palacký University Olomouc, Czech Republic

602   'Some people rather die of a gunshot than of hunger': How refugees
        in Northern Uganda negotiate the refugee label after targeted and
        reduced food assistance
        Roos Derrix, University of Antwerp, Belgium
        Milena Belloni, University of Antwerp, Belgium

957   Double Stigma: Making meaning of Religion in Understanding Young
        Muslim Migrants Experiences of Everyday Life in Norway
        *Memory Jayne Tembo-Pankuku, VID Specialised University,
        Norway*
        Ayan Handulle, University of Stavanger, Norway

516   Experiences of British Hosts: Reflections on the Hospitality Practices
        for Ukrainian Refugees
        Yael Gordon, London School of Economics and Political Science, UK

2E   Law, Policy and Governance 1   [Room: KW003]
Join via MS Teams
Moderator: Deniz Yetkin Aker, Istanbul Beykent University, Türkiye

2013   The Pact on Migration and Asylum and Changing Role of Frontex as
        European Border and Coast Guard Agency
        Deniz Yetkin Aker, Istanbul Beykent University, Türkiye
        Ismail Turan, Istanbul Beykent University, Türkiye

752   The administrative accountability of Frontex and the pioneering role
        of the European Ombudsman
        Alessio Laconi, University of Florence, Italy

833   State Power at Sea: Port Blockages, Legal Struggles, and the Politics
        of Migration Control
        *Sarah Elena Kruck, Goethe-University, Frankfurt am Main,
        Germany*

895   House Rules: Conceptualizing Norm Subversion within the Liberal
        International Order

Danielle Obisie-Orlu, Cornell University, USA

Join via MS Teams
Moderator: U. Sezgi Sozen, University of Hamburg, Germany

585   Experiences of Migrant Live-in Care Workers Facing the
       Death of Their Care Recipients
       Daniella Arieli, Emek Yezreel Academic College, Israel
       Gila Amitay, Emek Yezreel Academic College, Israel
       Dalit Yassour-Borochowitz, Emek Yezreel Academic College, Israel

657   Refugee Immigration and Crimes against Non-Refugee
       Foreigners
       Mohamad Alhussein Saoud, Otto-von-Guericke-University
       Magdeburg, Germany
       Michael Kvasnicka, Otto-von-Guericke-University Magdeburg,
       RWI, IZA, Germany

878   Fostering Empathy to Improve Migrant Integration in the
       Workforce (Part 1): Empathy in Critical Incidents Between
       German Employment Agents and Migrant Beneficiaries
       Saskia Judith Schubert, Berlin School of Economics and Law,
       Germany
       Carlotta Alpers, Berlin School of Economics and Law, Germany
       Tobias Ringeisen, Berlin School of Economics and Law, Germany

830   Comparing Reception Systems for Asylum Seekers: A participant
       observation in reception centers in Northern Italy
       Davide Carminati, X23 Science in Society, Italy
       Agathe Semlali, X23 Science in Society, France
       Cecilia Olivieri, X23 Science in Society, France

15:30 – 15:45: Break

11 June 2025, Wednesday
15:45 - 17:15
3A   Environment and Migration 2   [Room: KW302]

Join via MS Teams
Moderator: Nikola Lero, University of Sheffield, United Kingdom

707   Navigating the Nexus of International Migration Law, Climate Change,
       and Border Management: A Multidisciplinary Approach to Addressing
       Nigeria's Migration Challenges in the Context of Externalization and

Environmental Displacement
> *Grace Perpetual Dafiel, Veritas University Nigeria Abuja, Nigeria*
> *Ruqayyah Olaide Abdulaziz, University of Ilorin, Nigeria*
> *Comfort Onyanta Alli, Street Child Care and Welfare Initiative (SCCWI), Nigeria*

687 'Too Loud for Their Parks, Too Balkan for Their City': Transgenerational Domestic Homing, Urban Bordering, and the Aesthetics of Diasporic Nostalgia among Yugoslav-Serbs in London
> *Nikola Lero, University of Sheffield, United Kingdom*

835 The Limits of Law for Social Justice: Examining the Role of Law on Resource Extraction and Green Energy Development on Indigenous Peoples' Territory, and the Impact on their Rights, Livelihoods, and the Environment, in the Case of the Wayuu Indigenous People in Colombia
> *Pilar Balbuena, Carleton University, Canada*

3B   Education and Skilled Migration 3   [Room: KW303]

Join via MS Teams

Moderator: Lilach Lev Ari, Oranim Academic College of Education, Israel

590 Educators' perspectives on inclusive education of forced migrants' children in the Tel Aviv educational system
> *Lilach Lev Ari, Oranim Academic College of Education, Israel*
> *Laura Sigad, Oranim Academic College of Education , Israel*

614 Rincones de desahogo y risa: Playdate Pláticas with Immigrant Latina Grand/Mothers and their Children
> *Cathy de los Ríos, University of California, Berkeley, US*

501 Enhancing capabilities through education: educational and skills development for conflict-displaced Burmese youth in rural and urban Thailand
> *David Lefor, Ruhr University Bochum, Germany*

734 Support Immigrant Students in Schools
> *Lorena Tule-Romain, Southern Methodist University, USA*
> *Viridiana Carrizales, USA*

3C   Türkiye'de Göç 1 [Turkish]   [Room: KW315]

Join via MS Teams

Moderator: Filiz Göktuna Yaylacı, Anadolu University, Türkiye

528 "Kadın Başına Göç": Konya'daki Afgan Genç Kadınların Kaçış Hikayeleri ve Eril Şiddetle Mücadeleleri
> *Filiz Göktuna Yaylacı, Anadolu University, Türkiye*
> *Gamze Kaçar Tunç, Karamanoglu Mehmetbey University, Türkiye*

566   Anayasa Mahkemesinin Güncel Kararları ve Suriye'deki Rejim Değişikliği Sonrası Suriyelilerin Sınır Dışı Edilmesi
Hande Bingöl, İstanbul Üniversitesi, Türkiye

446   Göç Bağlamında İklim Mültecileri Tartışması ve Hukuki Çerçeve İhtiyacı
Şilan Merve Yeşilmen, Türkiye
Özge Çopuroğlu, Türkiye

538   Uluslararası Öğrenciler ve Uyum Süreçleri: Anadolu Üniversitesi Örneği
Filiz Göktuna Yaylacı, Anadolu University, Türkiye

3D   Law, Policy and Governance 2   [Room: KW002]

Join via MS Teams

Moderator: Deniz Yetkin Aker, Istanbul Beykent University, Türkiye

424   Navigating the Italian Refugee System: Legal Protections and Gaps
Alina Soloviova, European University Institute, Italy

750   Small State Responses to Migration Transformation: Baltic Regional Experience
Santa Barone-Upeniece, University of Latvia, Latvia

2009   Supporting Türkiye's Efforts for Efficient Migration Management
Emine Mermer Karaayak, IOM, Türkiye

842   The effectiveness of Due Process (or fair trial) of Irregular Subsaharan Migrants in Morocco: between Legal Framework and Practice (2003-2020)
Nabila Zouhiri, University Mohamed V - Souissi – Rabat, Morocco

3E   Environment and Migration 1   [Room: KW003]

Join via MS Teams

Moderator: Aniseh S. Bro, Appalachian State University, United States

467   Invisible communities: migrants in the wake of environmental disasters
Aniseh S. Bro, Appalachian State University, United States
Ellen Kraai,

831   Individual and Community Effects on Environmental Internal Migration Patterns in Senegal
Corentin Visée, University of Namur, Belgium
Sébastien Dujardin, University of Namur, Belgium
Sabine Henry, University of Namur, Belgium

686   Immigrant Women's Health in the Context of Climate and Social Justice: A Participatory Action Research Protocol
Fatemeh Khalaj, Laval University, Canada
Marie Pierre Gagnon, Laval University, Canada

Samira Amil, Laval University, Canada
Erika Corona, Laval University, Canada

564   Multi-layered Dynamics of Push and Pull Factors of Migration and its Changing Patterns in Coastal Bangladesh
Gazi Alif Laila, University of Leeds, United Kingdom
James Ford, University of Leeds, United Kingdom
Diana Ivanova, University of Leeds, United Kingdom
Jouni Paavola, University of Leeds, United Kingdom

3F   Wellbeing, Health and Migration 1 [Room: KW016]

Join via MS Teams

Moderator: Ana Vila-Freyer, Universidad de Guanajuato, México

864   Migration and Ageing in the South of Guanajuato, a case study
Ana Vila-Freyer, Universidad de Guanajuato, México

910   Stories Across Generations: A Meta-Synthesis of Intergenerational Trauma in Refugee Communities
Jaclyn Kirsch, University of Texas at Arlington, United States
Maryam Rafieifar, University of Texas at Arlington, United States
Hanna Haran, University of Texas at Arlington, United States

435   From Successful Start-Up to Sudden Collapse: What Predicts the Survival and Longevity of ICT-based Humanitarian Initiatives Designed to Help Refugees and Migrants?
Ziaul Haque, Juniata College, Pennsylvania, United States
Joseph G. Bock, Juniata College, United States

625   Preserving youth mental wellbeing in wartime migration crisis: Educators' reflection
Grazina Ciuladiene, Mykolas Romeris University, Lithuania
Nomeda Gudeliene, Mykolas Romeris University, Lithuania
Janina Ovcinikova, Mykolas Romeris University, Lithuania

12 June 2025, Thursday
09:00 - 10:30
4B   Law, Policy and Governance 3   [Room: KW302]

Join via MS Teams

Moderator: Radoslav Štefančík, University of Economics Bratislava, Slovakia

693   Participation of populists in government and its impact on migration discourse
Radoslav Štefančík, University of Economics Bratislava, Slovakia

548   How has the evolution of the liberal international order (LIO)

influenced the treatment of refugees in the Global North compared to the Global South?

> *Erin Gable, Boston University, USA*

841 Externalisation of Migration in the Reform of the Common European Asylum System: Legal Challenges and Human Rights Concerns

> *Katharina Stübinger, Università degli Studi di Palermo, Italy*

817 Positioning Turkey's Zafer Party in the Context of European Far-Right Parties' Discourses on Migrants: Is the Zafer Party a Far-Right Party?

> *Seher Atay, Suleyman Demirel University, Türkiye*
>
> *Ozlem Kahya Nizam, Suleyman Demirel University, Türkiye*

4C   Gender and Migration 3   [Room: KW315]

Join via MS Teams

Moderator: Fanny Margot Tudela Poblete, CA Actores Sociales y Desarrollo Comunitario, Belgium

628 "Las Patronas, la esperanza del migrante". Women's agency, experiences, and resiliences around transit migration

> *Fanny Margot Tudela Poblete, CA Actores Sociales y Desarrollo Comunitario, Belgium*
>
> *Jesus Madera Pacheco, Universidad Autonoma de Nayarit, Mexico*

787 "We are not objects!" - Contested remembrance using the example of Turkish-Greek forced migration

> *Anita Rotter, University of Innsbruck, Austria*

438 Migrant Women and Children Navigating and Transforming Migrantscapes: experiences and Situated Knowledge in Tijuana, Mexico

> *Frida Güiza, CETYS Universidad, Campus Tijuana, Mexico*
>
> *Haydee Beltran-Duran, Fundación Internacional de la Comunidad, Mexico*
>
> *Angela Serrano-Carrasco, Universidad Iberoamericana - Campus Tijuana, Mexico*

844 Constructing the Identity of Migrant Women in Transnational Marriages in South Korea: Challenging Stereotypical Media Representations

> *Jungmin Lee, Ecole des Hautes Etudes en Sciences Sociales, France*

4D   Space, Place and Migration 1   [Room: KW002]

Join via MS Teams

Moderator: T. Elizabeth Durden, Bucknell University, USA

839 Growing Acceptance: Farmers Market and Immigrant Inclusion in

New Destinations
T. Elizabeth Durden, Bucknell University, USA

635 Expected Identities: Tibetans in-exile and the pressures of "Tibetan-ness"
Jack Michael McMahon, University of Melbourne, Australia

736 Everyday experiences of refugees: A Participatory Photographic Study in Paris, Vienna, and Madrid
Johanna Laetizia Exenberger, Université Paris Cité, France

868 Constructing Hungarian Heterotopia: German-speaking Lifestyle Migrants and Western Disillusionment
Philipp Kuhn, University of Szeged, Hungary
Gábor Hegedűs, University of Szeged, Hungary

4E   Work, Employment and Society 2   [Room: KW003]

Join via MS Teams

Moderator: Emily Bergner, Radboud University, Netherlands

646 From Demographic Reproduction to Social Stratification. Migration and the reconfiguration of social classes in Catalonia in the XXI century
Carlos Ruiz-Ramos, Centre for Demographic Studies (CED-CERCA) and Universitat Autònoma de Barcelona, Spain
Andreu Domingo, Centre for Demographic Studies (CED-CERCA), Spain
Rocío Treviño, Centre for Demographic Studies (CED-CERCA), Spain

806 Syrian refugees and their entrance in the Austrian labour market: Comparison of different arrival cohorts
Isabella Buber-Ennser, Austrian Academy of Sciences, Austria
Bernhard Rengs, Austria
Judith Kohlenberger, Vienna University of Economics and Business, Austria
Sophie Reichelt, Austrian Institute for International Affairs, Austria

879 Fostering Empathy to Improve Migrant Integration in the Workforce (Part 2): Designing a Training Program for Employment Agents
Carlotta Alpers, Berlin School of Economics and Law, Germany
Saskia Schubert, Berlin School of Economics and Law, Germany
Tobias Ringeisen, Berlin School of Economics and Law, Germany

527 A comparative study on the labour market outcomes of internal and international migrants in Ecuador
Emily Bergner, Radboud University, Netherlands
Nicole Salazar Alvarez, Netherlands

Jimena Pacheco, Leiden University, Netherlands
Natascha Wagner, Radboud University, Netherlands

4F   Theory, Data and Methods 1   [Room: KW016]
Join via MS Teams

Moderator: *Sureyya Sonmez Efe, University of Lincoln, United Kingdom*

822   Quantifying Social Capital: A Formal Methodology for the Analysis of Access to Information While on the Move
Andrew Fallone, University of Cambridge, United Kingdom

885   Transnational Gentrification in Sicily: Lifestyle Migrants and Inequality
Valeria Holguin Arcia, Universita di Catania, Italy

396   Predicting Migration: The Human Rights Implications of the EU's Ubiquitous Border
Giovanni Dini, Universitat Autònoma de Barcelona / Institut Barcelona d'Estudis Internacionals, Spain

751   Photovoice Methodology and Representation of Refugee Women: Nuanced Understanding of Lived Experiences of Maternal Care Services in Türkiye
Sureyya Sonmez Efe, University of Lincoln, United Kingdom

10:30 – 10:45: Break

12 June 2025, Thursday
10:45 - 12:15
5A   Theory, Data and Methods 2   [Room: KW302]
Join via MS Teams

Moderator: *Ali Faruk Yaylacı, Kütahya Dumlupınar University, Türkiye*

675   Co-construction of a Sensitization Workshop on Culturally Responsive Teaching: Facilitators and Obstacles to Collaboration with Secondary School Teachers
Corinne Hébert, Université de Montréal, Canada
Isabelle Archambault, Université de Montréal, Canada
Kristel Tardif-Grenier, Université du Québec en Outaouais, Canada

715   Regional multistate projection of future inequalities: Migration and educational attainment in Spanish regions 2024-2074
Osama Damoun, Centre for Demographic Studies (CED), Barcelona, Spain
Dilek Yildiz, International Institute for Applied Systems Analysis

(IIASA), Austria

876　Rootedness and a Culture of Staying Amidst Out Migration in Rural Guatemala
　　　Helen Hobson, Kennesaw State University, USA

911　A Conceptualization of School Citizenship for the New Citizens of Schools in Türkiye: The Rights and Responsibilities of Immigrant/Refugee Students and Parents
　　　Ali Faruk Yaylacı, Kütahya Dumlupınar University, Türkiye

5B　Arts, Literature, Media 3　[Room: KW303]

Join via MS Teams

Moderator:　Lan Lo, University of Nottingham, United Kingdom

738　'We' as a place of refuge in the 'New Migration Crónica'
　　　Irene Praga Guerro, Birkbeck College, University of London, United Kingdom

624　"Broken mirrors": the temporalities of post migration in contemporary British literature
　　　Juliana Lopoukhine, Sorbonne University, Paris, France

427　Fallen leaves, new roots: burial places of the Chinese diaspora
　　　Kellin Wang, United Kingdom

907　Talking Trees / 树说/述说：home, paths, roots, and the metaphorical growth of trees across time for a sense of belonging
　　　Lan Lo, University of Nottingham, United Kingdom

5C　Business, Economics, Development 1　[Room: KW315]

Join via MS Teams

Moderator: Aytaç Uğur Yerden, Istanbul Gedik University, Türkiye

936　Support Mechanisms for Business Creation in the Walloon Region for non-European Migrants
　　　Honorine Kuete, University of Mons, Belgium

737　Exit Taxes as a Barrier to Emigration and The Need for an International Treaty To Create Uniformity and Certainty Surrounding Emigration
　　　John Richardson, SEAT - "Stop Extraterritorial American Taxation" - SEATNow.org, Canada

660　Reverse Hawala: Unveiling the Role of Informal Remittance Systems in Trade Finance Between Turkey and Afghanistan
　　　Mohammad Ayoub Babur, Karadeniz Technical University, Türkiye

2002　A Research on the Effect of Digital Immigrants' and Digital Natives'

Attitudes Towards Innovation on Their Purchase Intentions
Nevin Karabiyik Yerden, Marmara University, Türkiye
Aytaç Uğur Yerden, Istanbul Gedik University, Türkiye

5D   Law, Policy and Governance 4   [Room: KW002]

Join via MS Teams

Moderator: Laura Snyder, Association of Americans Resident Overseas (AARO); Stop Extraterritorial American Taxation (SEAT), France

623   Refusing to Let Go: A Tale of Two Emigrations
Laura Snyder, Association of Americans Resident Overseas (AARO); Stop Extraterritorial American Taxation (SEAT), France

798   Syrian Refugee Children's Voice in the United States of America: A Call for Increased Participation in Migration Processes
Emily Kwok, Macquarie University, Australia

421   Claiming Belonging and Rationalizing Restrictiveness: The Evolution of Asylum Seekers' Legal Consciousness in the Context of Reception
Laura Rakotomalala, Free University of Brussels, Belgium

748   Uncertainties upon Uncertainties: An Ethnographic Research on the Migration Experiences of British National (Overseas) Migrants in the UK
Lok Yee Liona Li, International Institute of Social Studies, Netherlands

5E   Integration and Migration 3   [Room: KW003]

Join via MS Teams

Moderator: Ritika Tanotra, York University, Canada

773   Faith-based Transnationalism: Transnational Religious Experiences Connecting Filipino Migrant Workers in Singapore and their Left-behind Families in the Philippines
Evangeline O. Katigbak-Montoya, De La Salle University Manila, Philippines

651   Forgiveness and grudge as affective orientations towards the future amongst Hungarian and Venezuelan migrants in London
Judit Molnar, University of Oxford, United Kingdom

444   Redefining Resentment: Growing Anti-Immigration Rhetoric and Racism Towards Indian South Asians in Canada
Ritika Tanotra, York University, Canada

765   The Right to Have Rights for "Arendt's Children": The Conceptual and Policy Predicament
Yuri Keum, Ben-Gurion University of the Negev, Israel

5F   Space, Place and Migration 2 [Room: KW016]

Join via MS Teams

Moderator: Ibrahim Sirkeci, International Business School, Manchester, UK

814   Beyond Migration: Exploring Young People's (Im)Mobility and the Good Life in Brazil
Adélia Verônica da Silva, University of Lisbon, Portugal
Maria Lucinda Fonseca, University of Lisbon, Portugal

789   Biographical Narratives in the Postmigrant Urban Society: The Example of London
Anita Rotter, University of Innsbruck, Austria

603   The Emergence of Second Generations in Spain: A Geographic Analysis at Different Scales in the Province of Barcelona
Jordi Bayona-i-Carrasco, Universitat de Barcelona, Spain
Andreu Domingo, Centre d'Estudis Demogràficcs, Spain
Nachatter Singh, Universidade da Coruña, Spain

937   The Law that Targeted a Group: Immigration Law in Costa Rica and its impact on Nicaraguan immigrants
Julissa Maria Ramirez Perez, University of South Florida, USA

12:15 – 13:15: Lunch Break

12 June 2025, Thursday
13:15 - 14:45
Plenary Discussion Session:
"Migration Policy Challenges in the New Era of Uncertainty"
[Room: KW303 – King William Building, 3rd Floor]

Join via MS Teams

Keynote Speakers:
*Emeritus Professor Philip L. **Martin**, University of California Davis, USA*
*Professor Ozlem **Onaran**, University of Greenwich, UK*
*Discussant: Professor Jeffrey H. **Cohen**, Ohio State University, USA*

14:45 – 15:00: Break

6A   Theory and Methods 3 [Room: KW302]

Join via MS Teams

Moderator: Klement R. Camaj, University of the West of Scotland, UK

431   Redefining Diaspora – A Modern Outlook to a Classical Concept
Klement R. Camaj, University of the West of Scotland, UK
Murray Leith, University of the West of Scotland, UK

754   Tracing the 'Biosecurity-Immigration Nexus': The Extension of Biosecurity into the Canadian Immigration Regime Since the COVID-19 Pandemic
Pablo Roy-Rojas, York University, Canada

619   Have we been Measuring Migrant Wellbeing all Wrong? Conceptualizing Migrant Wellbeing: A Systematic Review
Salsawi Feleke Debela, University of Melbourne, Australia
Sheenagh McShane, University of Melbourne, Australia
Lauren Carpenter, University of Melbourne, Australia
Celia McMichael, University of Melbourne, Australia
Ankur Singh, University of Melbourne, Australia
Karen Block, University of Melbourne, Australia

425   E pluribus unum? Redefining the Main Premises of Acculturation Theory and Testing Them as a Unified Model
Eugene Tartakovsky, Tel Aviv University, Israel

6B   Law, Policy and Governance 5   [Room: KW303]

Join via MS Teams

Moderator: Li Zeming, City University of Hong Kong, China

685   Explaining the Indian State's Policy Response to Female Migrant Domestic Workers
Patrick R Ireland, Illinois Institute of Technology, USA

605   Demography and Democracy: Navigating the European Union's Migration Maze
Andreu Domingo-Valls, Autonomous Universuty of Barcelona, Spain
Gemma Pinyol, Pompeu Fabra University, Spain

649   The Impact of the Best Interests Principle on the Protection of Migrant Children: the Views of the Committee on the Rights of the Child
Jaroslav Větrovský, Palacký University, Czech Republic

545   Political Realism and Historical Continuity: Analyzing China's Evolving

Framework for Refugee Management
Li Zeming, City University of Hong Kong, China

6C Wellbeing, Health and Migration 2 [Room: KW315]

Join via MS Teams

Moderator: Jocelyn O. Celero, University of the Philippines Diliman

690 Public Attitudes Toward Publicly Funded Health Care Access for Non-Citizens: A Cross-National Analysis
Claire Ardell Pernat, Boston University School of Public Health, USA

803 Intersectional inequalities, well-being, and migration: a scoping review
Margarida Martins Barroso, UNED, Spain

776 What explains migrants' resilience during reintegration? Examining the returned overseas Filipino workers' experience during the COVID-19 pandemic
Melissa R. Garabiles, De La Salle University and Scalabrini Migration Center, Philippines
Maruja Milagros B. Asis, Scalabrini Migration Center and International Organization for Migration Philippines, Philippines

418 Have you Heard from Migrant/Ethnic Minority Parents Raising Children with Disabilities?
Noah Agbo, Queen's University Belfast, United Kingdom

6D Integration and Migration 4 [Room: KW002]

Join via MS Teams

Moderator: Michela C. Pellicani, University of Bari, Italy

721 International migrants in Switzerland: comparing the trajectories and outcomes of migrants from EU and non-EU countries
Justyna Salamonska, Kozminski University, Poland

591 Eritrean Forced Migrants in Tel Aviv: Between Social Integration and Exclusion
Lilach Lev Ari, Oranim Academic College of Education, Israel
Arie Herscovici, Western Galilee College, Israel

498 Minority Groups in Academia: Identity, Challenges, and Opportunities
Adi Binhas, Beit Berl College, Israel

735 Feminist Networks of Solidarity in the US-Mexico Borderlands
Ayden Jordan Cox, Queens University Belfast, USA

393 Reintegration and Resilience among returnees
Ammar Saeed Ammar, American University of Beirut (AUB), Lebanon

6E   Gender and Migration 2   [Room: KW003]

Join via MS Teams

Moderator: Tahire Erman, Bilkent University, Türkiye

977   Navigating Patriarchy in the Humanitarian Field: Syrian
         Refugee Women in a Slum Neighborhood in Ankara, Türkiye
                 Tahire Erman, Bilkent University, Türkiye

912   Exploring conceptions of 'Home' with Afghan migrant and
         refugee women
                 Rabia Nasimi, Cambridge University, United Kingdom

971   Gendered Precarity: Exploring the Experiences of Women
         Temporary Migrant Farm Workers in Québec, Canada
                 Roxanne Fay, University of Sherbrooke, Québec, Canada

898   Luchando Junt@s Por Una Familia Unida (Fighting Together for a
         United Family): Rebuilding the Cohesive Self of Immigrant Parents
         and Community Healing after a Family Separation in the United
         States – A Self Psychology Perspective
                 Cheryl Aguilar, Smith College, USA

6F   Sponsor Workshop: Immigration Pathways to Canada
[Room: KW016]

Join via MS Teams

This is a special session run by InterCan Solutions. Postgraduate students,
Master or Doctoral, are invited to join.

16:30 – 16:45: Break

12 June 2025, Thursday
16:30 - 18:00

7X   National Maritime Museum – Migration Related Object Tour
[Lecture Theatre of the National Maritime Museum]

National Maritime Museum - Migration Related Object Tour
>>> **Free booking required:** Please book via this link:
https://tickets.rmg.co.uk/webstore/shop/viewItems.aspx?cg=MIOT&c
=MIOTC

7A   Youth Migration 1   [Room: KW302]

Join via MS Teams

Moderator: Liat Yakhnich, Beit Berl College, Israel

811   Beyond the Return Myth: Young Brazilian Migrants in Portugal and the (Im)mobility Paradox

Adélia Verônica da Silva, University of Lisbon, Portugal

Maria Lucinda Fonseca, University of Lisbon, Portugal

586   Unaccompanied Migrant Minors' governance: a Pendulum between Protection and Control. Comparative analysis among democratic systems in U.S. and EU

Isabella Miano, University of Catania, Italy

783   Aging Out: Examining the Mental Health and Social Service Needs of Unaccompanied Immigrant Youth during the Precarious Transition to Adulthood

Kristina K. Lovato, University of California, Berkeley, USA

463   Immigrant Youth from France in Israel: Adaptation and Risk Behaviours

Liat Yakhnich, Beit Berl College, Israel

Keren Michael, Max Stern Yezreel Valley College, Israel

7B   Wellbeing, Health and Migration 3   [Room: KW303]

Join via MS Teams

Moderator: Ana Vila-Freyer, Universidad de Guanajuato, México

692   Understanding Vaccination Gaps: A Nativity-Based Analysis of COVID-19 and Flu Vaccine Uptake in the United States

Claire Ardell Pernat, Boston University, USA

Matthew Motta, Boston University, USA

555   Determinants of Access to Private Health Insurance or Medicare Among Mexican Immigrant Heads of Households in Chicago

Jose M. Soltero, DePaul University, USA

606   Scarcity in Crises – The Role of Personal Resources in Accessing COVID-19 Vaccines in Germany

Laura Goßner, Institute for Employment Research (IAB), Germany

733   Empowered and Healthy Immigrant Families: Piloting an SDOH Curriculum

Claudia M. Castillo-Lavergne, Rutgers Graduate School of Applied & Professional Psychology, USA

German Cadenas, Rutgers Graduate School of Applied &
Professional Psychology, USA
Lorena Tule-Romain, ImmSchools, USA
Viridiana Carrizales, ImmSchools, USA

664 The challenges of digital health training for pregnant immigrant
women in the perinatal process. Evaluation of the COLINE project
Erika Corona Velazquez, Laval University, Canada
Marielle M'bangha, Perinatal Care Reference Service for Migrant
Women from Quebec, Canada
Marie-Pierre Gagnon, Laval University, Canada

7C   Law, Policy and Governance 6   [Room: KW315]
Join via MS Teams

Moderator: Karelys Guzmán, Central Bank of Colombia,
Colombia

867 Venezuelan migration shock in Colombia and its fiscal implications for
the health sector at the local level
Karelys Guzmán, Central Bank of Colombia, Colombia

809 Analyzing the Experiences of Filipino Undocumented Deportees from
Sabah: A Framework for Bilateral Support between the Philippines and
Malaysia
Renante C. David, Polytechnic University of the Philippines,
Philippines
Ramli Dollah, Universiti of Malaysia Sabah, Malaysia

652 The Latin-American contribution for a human rights-based mobility
regime: Argentinean and Mexican Supreme Courts' standards in
perspective
Lila Emilse Garcia, CONICET & Leuphana Universitat, Argentina

795 Refugee Status Determination Policy and Practice: Why the "zero-boats"
Australian Migration Policy Resulted in Increased Asylum Seekers?
Petra Madge Playfair, PLAYFAIR Visa and Migration Services,
Australia

7D   Integration and Migration 5   [Room: KW002]
Join via MS Teams

Moderator: Stacey Wilson-Forsberg, Wilfrid Laurier University, Canada

788 Responding to the Ukrainian refugee crisis in Hungary and Austria: space
for social innovation?
Julianna Kiss, Corvinus University of Budapest, Hungary
Henriett Primecz, Johannes Kepler University, Linz, Austria

Jeannine Madeleine Ölschuster, Johannes Kepler University, Austria

650   Adaptation and Integration of Ukrainian Refugees: Problems and Challenges, Social Assistance, Plans for the Future (Germany, Italy, Poland, and the United Kingdom)
Liudmyla Kryvachuk, University of the National Education Commission of Cracow, Poland

470   Collective Integration Experiences of Refugee Women and their Networks
Siobhan C. McEvoy, University College Dublin, Republic of Ireland
Laura K. Taylor, University College Dublin, Republic of Ireland

554   Empowering Mothers from the Horn of Africa to Engage with their Children's Schools
Stacey Wilson-Forsberg, Wilfrid Laurier University, Canada
Mohamed Bille Hassan, Guelph University, Canada
Oliver Masakure, Wilfrid Laurier University, Canada

7E   Work, Employment and Society 3   [Room: KW003]

Join via MS Teams

Moderator: Anna Benice Xavier, Deakin University, Australia

703   Challenging the stereotypical perception of emigration agents in post-unification Italy: an archival excavation into Sicilian sources
Alice Gussoni, University of Padua, Italy

2001   Empowering Refugees: Promoting Labour Market Integration through Career Clinics for Meaningful Employment
Anna Benice Xavier, Deakin University, Australia
Karen Dunwoodie, Deakin University, Australia

511   The Employment Experiences of Black Personal Support Workers in Ontario, Canada
Bharati Sethi, Trent University, Canada
Reemal Shahbaz, University of Toronto, Canada
Sarrah Williams-Habibi, Stanford University, USA
Allison Williams and Albert Larbi

697   The Relevance of Occupational Mobility for Seasonal Labour Migrants: Insights from Switzerland's AFMP Implementation
Livia Tomás, ZHAW School of Social Work, Institute of Diversity and Social Integration & University of Neuchâtel, Switzerland
Kristina Schüpbach, ETH Zurich, KOF Swiss Economic Institute, Switzerland

Join via MS Teams

Moderator: Susanne Buckley-Zistel, Philipps University Marburg, Germany

2029   Humanrightization of Migration Discourses
        Susanne Buckley-Zistel, Philipps University Marburg, Germany

2030   Translating Experience into Political Resistance: Human Rights
        Discourse in Refugee and Migrant Struggle Against Politics of
        Isolation
        *Encarnación Gutiérrez Rodríguez, Goethe University Frankfurt,
        Germany*
        Slađana Branković, Goethe University Frankfurt, Germany

2031   The Effects of Humanitarian Tropes on Representation of Migrants in
        Legacy and Digital Media
        Simona Adinolfi, Justus Liebig University Giessen, Germany

2032   How Human Rights Can Change Domestic Migration Law: The
        Example of Germany
        Frederik von Harbou, University of Applied Sciences Jena, Germany

2033   Diasporic Consciousness in Postrevolutionary Times - On Syrian
        Justice Struggles in Germany
        Maria Hartmann, University of Marburg, Germany

12 June 2025, Thursday
19:30 - 22:00
CONFERENCE GALA DINNER
The Old Brewery, Greenwich, The Pepys Building, The Old Royal Naval College
Greenwich, London SE10 9LW
Tel. 020 3437 2222
Directions: Google Map

13 June 2025, Friday
09:00 - 13:00

FREE TIME

Join via MS Teams

Moderator: Alfonso Mercado, University of Texas Rio Grande Valley, USA

600   Drawing Strengths: Trauma-informed expressive arts for asylum-seeking children in a humanitarian respite center at the US-Mexico border

Alfonso Mercado, University of Texas Rio Grande Valley, USA
Kim Nguyen-Finn, University of Texas Rio Grande Valley, USA
Cecilia Garza, University of Texas Rio Grande Valley, USA
Andy Torres, University of Texas Rio Grande Valley, USA
Francisco Banda, University of Texas Rio Grande Valley, USA
Erin Tovar, University of Texas Rio Grande Valley, USA
Ricardo Robles, University of Texas Rio Grande Valley, USA

691   Foreign-Born Disparities in Cervical Cancer Screening: How Education and Insurance Shape Utilization

Claire Ardell Pernat, Boston University, USA
Matthew Motta, Boston University, USA

2036   A Grounded Theory Exploration of wellbeing and liveable space for Uganda-based refugee women, forcibly displaced due to conflict

Helen Harrison, University of Gloucestershire, UK

893   What About the Parents? Exploring the Impact of Immigration Family Separation on the Wellbeing and Sense of Self Among Central American Parents

Cheryl Aguilar, Smith College, USA

8B   Integration and Migration 6   [Room: KW303]

Join via MS Teams

Moderator: Apostolos G. Papadopoulos, Harokopio University, Greece

882   Integration and civic society in Italy

Mariann Dömös, University of Pécs, Hungary

500   The Relationship Between Attitudes Toward Immigrants, Ethnic Identity and Bullying Perpetration Among Immigrant and Non-Immigrant Adolescents in Israel: A Multi-Level Study

Sophie D. Walsh, Bar Ilan University, Israel
Anna Gliklich, Bar Ilan University, Israel

976   'In/out of place': Shedding light on ethnic hierarchies and

lived experiences of racism in rural Greece
> *Loukia – Maria Fratsea, Harokopio University, Greece*
> *Apostolos G. Papadopoulos, Harokopio University, Greece*

8C   Special Session: Migrants Navigating the Liminal: Cultural Heritage, Resilience and Representation   [Room: KW315]

Join via MS Teams

Moderator: Neveen Aboueldahab, Ibnhaldun University, Türkiye

2027   Digital Spaces and Self-Representation: Migrant Women's Voices in Türkiye's Social Media
> *Nurefsan Celenk, Ibnhaldun University, Türkiye*

2028   "Like Those Who Dance in Stairwells": Navigating Ruptures, Liminality & Imaginaries in Exilic Filmmaking
> *Mariam Agha, Ibnhaldun University, Türkiye*

2026   Resilience in the Face of Marginalization: Arab Migrants' Cultural Heritage and Recovery Through Art and Socio-Cultural Practices in Turkey
> *Neveen Aboueldahab, Ibnhaldun University, Türkiye*

542   Security and Adaptation: The Polish Diaspora Experience in Türkiye
> *Gizem Karaköse, Nicolaus Copernicus University, Poland*

8D   Youth and Migration 2   [Room: KW002]

Join via MS Teams

Moderator: Şeyma Ayyıldız, Boğaziçi University, Türkiye

671   New Challenges of Youth Migration from Central Asia to Russia
> *Liudmila Konstants, American University of Central Asia, Kyrgyzstan*

857   Barriers and Motivations for youth development professionals in the U.S. to engage youth with an immigrant background
> *Mitchell Mason, University of Maine – Orono, USA*

821   Determinants of mental health and wellbeing for young migrant populations: A scoping review
> *Melanie Rees-Roberts, University of Kent, UK*
> *Palmira Ramos, UK*
> *Jade Fawkes, UK*
> *Dunishiya De Silva, University of Kent, UK*
> *Oluwatomi Shobande, Project public advisor – expert by experience*
> *Francesca Gan, Project public advisor – expert by experience*
> *Sally Kendall, University of Kent, UK*

492   Spatial Functions of Multiple Temporalities: The Case of Syrian
      Students in Istanbul
          Şeyma Ayyıldız, Boğaziçi University, Türkiye

**8E   Special Session: From Aspiration to Integration: Vietnamese
Students' Mobility to the Global North
[Room: KW003]**
Join via MS Teams
Moderator: Anh Phuong Le, Waseda University, Japan
2019 False Perceptions and Lived Experiences of Vietnamese
      Students in Canada
          Quang Minh Huyn, Simon Fraser University, Canada
2020 "Influenced Factors and the Precarity of Vietnamese
      Students in Ireland
          Trinh Thien Kim Nguyen, University College Dublin, Ireland
2022 From Student Migrants to Dual Nationalities: Higher
      Education as a Mediator for Immigration and Integration -
      The Case of Vietnamese in Finland
          Hai Yen Nguyen, Finland
2021 From International Students to Specified Skilled Workers:
      Vietnamese Students' Post-graduation Pathway to the
      Japanese Manual Labour Market
          Anh Phuong Le, Waseda University, Japan

14:30 – 14:45: Break

13 June 2025, Friday
14:45 – 16:15
9A   Wellbeing, Health and Migration 5 [Room: KW302]
Join via MS Teams
Moderator: Alfonso Mercado, University of Texas Rio Grande Valley, USA
688   Stressors of Emotional/Behavioral Problems Among Different
      Members in Immigrant Families in Taiwan
          Hao-Jan Yang, Chung Shan Medical University, Taiwan
          Wan-Yi Dai, Chung Shan Medical University, Taiwan
866   The Psychological Toll of Migration: Factors Influencing Trauma in
      Asylum Seekers at the U.S.-Mexico Border
          Renee M. Frederick, University of Houston, USA
          Ashley Bautista, University of Houston, USA

Daniel O'Connell, University of Houston, USA
Luz Garcini, Rice University, USA
Alfonso Mercado, University of Texas Rio Grande Valley, USA
Cecilia Colunga Rodriguez, University of Guadalajara, Mexico
Mario Angel Gonzalez, University of Guadalajara, Mexico
Amanda Venta, University of Houston, USA

413   Narcissistic parenting, psychological well-being and the achievement of emerging adult tasks within the context of immigration
Katya Ben Efraim, Bar-Ilan University, Israel
Sophie Walsh, Bar-Ilan University, Israel

9B   Integration and Migration 7   [Room: KW303]

Join via MS Teams

Moderator: Gizem Karaköse, Nicolaus Copernicus University, Poland

705   Asylum Seeker Presence and Community Support: Do Asylum Seeker Hotels Influence Donations to Refugee Charities?
Sophia M. Iosue, Bocconi University, Italy

799   Reconsidering Citizenship: Cultural Claims and Social Practices in the Migrant Experience
Stefano Pontiggia, Politecnico di Milano, Italy

732   Exploitation of migrant workers in a peripheral area of Italy. Methodological proposals to de-construct Italian migration policies and the Italian citizenship regime for migrants
Norma Baldino, University of Cagliari, Italy
Sabrina Perra, University of Cagliari, Italy

518   Inclusive Narratives, Exclusionary Realities: Examining Diversity, Marginality, and Social Complexity in East London
Tamlyn Monson, Coventry University, United Kingdom
Susanne Wessendorf, Coventry University, United Kingdom

9C   Migration and Insecurity   [Room: KW315]

Join via MS Teams

Moderator: Nonna Kushnirovich, Ruppin Academic Center, Israel

727   The Dynamics of Tax Morale: A Comparative Study of Immigrants and Native-Born Citizens
Nonna Kushnirovich, Ruppin Academic Center, Israel

764   Migration, Conflicts, and Governance Considerations in Water-Energy-Food Systems
Konstantinos Pappas, Texas A&M University, USA

922   Border Metaphors--From Crisis to Invasion: The Securitization of the

Border in Response to Irregular Migration
DeMond Shondell Miller, Rowan University, USA
Anita D. Bledsoe-Gardner, Johnson C. Smith University, USA
887 Invisible walls: A representation of everyday borders in the experience of asylum seekers through the effect of the asylum system in the UK
Sarah Elmammeri, University of Liverpool, UK

9D Integración y Migración [Room: KW002]

Join via MS Teams

Moderator: Karla Valenzuela, Iberoamericana University, Mexico
854 Migración de talentos del Magreb Central: Argelia en el punto de mira
Hadibi Zahir, University of Bejaia, Algeria
Musette Yasmine, CREAD, Algiers, Algeria
568 Migración de retorno a Michoacán de Estados Unidos y la construcción de un programa de coinversión social para su integración económica, comunitaria y familiar
Karina Raquel Zúñiga Delgado, Universidad Autónoma de Zacatecas, México
Rodolfo García Zamora, Universidad Autónoma de Zacatecas, México
792 Lives in Transit: Stories of Refugees
Priyali Sur, The Azadi Project, India
Ankita Dan, The Azadi Project, India

13 June 2025, Friday
14:45 - 16:15
9E   Roundtable: Food Security among Afghan Refugees
[Room: KW003]
Join via MS Teams

A special session where the lead investigators from a multi-country study will share their insight on the quality of life and food security status of Afghan refugees after Taliban takeover in Iran, Canada and the US while exploring the well-being of residents in Afghanistan.

*Chair: Hassan **Vatanparast**, University of Saskatchewan, Canada*
Panellists:
*- Mohammad Reza **Pakravan-Charvadeh**, Lorestan University, Iran*
*- Ginny **Lane**, University of Idaho, USA*
*- Rasoul **Sadeghi**, University of Tehran, Iran*
*- Nasrin **Omidvar**, Shahid Beheshti University of Medical Sciences, Iran*

Q&A

16:15 – 16:30: Break

13 June 2025, Friday
16:30 – 18:00
10A   Work, Employment and Society 4   [Room: KW302]
Join via MS Teams

Moderator: Wenfu Zhang, University of Warwick, UK

543   Internal Migration, Employment and Remittances: A Study of Migrants from Tribal-Dominated Northeastern States in Delhi, India
Gaidimlung Kahmei Jacob, National Institute of Public Finance and Policy (NIPFP), New Delhi, Ministry of Finance, Government of India

399   The Puerto Rican Diaspora's Return Dilemma
Marielys Padua Soto, The American University in Cairo, Egypt

712   Empowering Asylum Seekers Through NGOs Volunteerism in Hong Kong
Kim, Minoh, The Chinese University of Hong Kong, Hong Kong
Liu, Bowei, The Chinese University of Hong Kong, Hong Kong
Xu, Junhao, The Chinese University of Hong Kong, Hong Kong
Zheng, Yichun, The Chinese University of Hong Kong, Hong Kong

458   Chinese Übermensches: Mobility Capital and the Entrepreneurial

46

Experiences of Young Privileged Chinese Migrants
Wenfu Zhang, University of Warwick, UK

10B   Law, Policy and Governance 7   [Room: KW303]

Join via MS Teams

Moderator: Gizem Karaköse, Nicolaus Copernicus University, Poland

567   Multilingual Practices and Linguistic Realities in Migration Studies
Gizem Karaköse, Nicolaus Copernicus University, Poland

901   Contingency Accommodation, Relocation, and Integration:
Understanding Asylum   Seekers' Experiences of Control,
'Temporariness', and Displacement
Fariba Alamgir, University of East Anglia, UK

720   The Influence of Socio-Demographic Factors and Municipal Political
Contexts on Foreign Voter Registration for the 2024 Local Elections in
Brussels
Gabriel Feddern Timm, Université Libre de Bruxelles, Belgium

909   Lived Diversity in Germany's Migration Landscape: Interactions
Between Turkey-Origin Residents and Post-2015 'Muslim' Immigrants
Melisa Çelik, University of Münster, Germany

10C   Integration and Migration 8   [Room: KW315]

Join via MS Teams

Moderator: Michela C. Pellicani, University of Bari, Italy

730   "People on Twitter are saying": Digital constructions of refugees in
Turkey
Emma Walker-Silverman, University of Oxford, United Kingdom

587   Privilege and Dichotomy: North American Immigrants' Experiences in
the Czech Republic as Counternarratives of Migration
Madeline Paradise, Masaryk University, Czech Republic

2012   Integration: Processes, Potential, and Policies at the Territorial Level
Michela C. Pellicani, University of Bari, Italy
Monica Carbonara, ISTAT, Italy
Roberto A. Palumbo, ISTAT, Italy
Massimo Iaquinta, University of Bari, Italy

990   Migration and Housing: Changing Dynamics in Turkey
Volkan Öngel, Beykent University, Turkey
Gözde Bozkurt, Beykent University, Turkey

10D   Special session: Mexico as a destination country: a new reality? [English/Español]   [Room: KW002]

Join via MS Teams

Moderator: Karla Valenzuela, Iberoamericana University, Mexico

2004   Landscape of federal and local integration policies in Mexico
          Karla Valenzuela, Iberoamericana University, Mexico

2006   Detention of Migrants and Human Rights: Perspectives Amid
          Presidential Transitions in Mexico and the U.S.
          Ariadna Salazar Quiñones, Iberoamericana University, Mexico

2007   Los indeseables: migrantes en campamentos irregulares en la ciudad
          de México
          Cristina Gómez Johnson, Iberoamericana University, Mexico

2008   Militarización y criminalización: la respuesta de México a las personas
          migrantes ante las presiones de Estados Unidos
          Margarita Núñez Chaim, Iberoamericana University, Mexico

13 June 2025, Friday
18:00 - 18:30

**11XA Drinks Reception and Migration Film Screening with Artists
        [Lecture Theatre of the National Maritime Museum]**

>>> Free booking required: https://www.rmg.co.uk/whats-on/national-maritime-museum/maritime-migration-film-screenings-panel-discussion-refugee-week

18:30 - 20:30

**11XB Migration Film Screening with Artists
        [Lecture Theatre of the National Maritime Museum]**

Liquid Traces: The Left-to-Die Boat Case

Liquid Traces reconstructs the events of the "left-to-die" boat case. In March 2011, a small rubber boat carrying 72 passengers left the Libyan coast, heading towards the island of Lampedusa in Italy.

Following an engine failure, the boat ran into difficulties. Despite several distress signals relaying the location, and encounters with military helicopters and ships, the passengers were left adrift for 14 days in NATO's maritime surveillance area. 63 people died.

This short film is directed by Charles Heller and Lorenzo Pezzani.

The Story of Migration

This short, animated film explores the relationship between migration and inequality. It was crated by Karrie Fransman for research organisation PositiveNegatives, and was nominated for 'Best Animated Film' in the Arts and Humanities Research Council's Research in Film Awards 2021.

Life on the Move

Centred on the Horn of Africa, this stop-motion animation explores the complex reasons why people move across borders, drawing on migrant experiences. Created by PositiveNegatives, the film was the winner of the 'Best Social Media Short' category in the Arts and Humanities Research Council's Research in Film Awards 2019.
The film was directed by Osbert Parker and Dr Benjamin Worku-Dix. Please be aware that it contains depictions of violence.

Artists to join us:
Dr Benjamin Worku-Dix *is the Founding Director of PositiveNegatives and a Senior Fellow at SOAS, University of London.*
Shorsh Saleh *is an artist. His works focus on the subjects of migration and identity, employing the traditional techniques of miniature painting in a contemporary context. His work "Crossing Border", has recently been acquired by Royal Museums Greenwich.*
Güler Ateş *was born in Eastern Turkey and lives and works in the UK. Her multidisciplinary work encompasses video, photography, printmaking and performance through which she explores the experience of identity, diaspora and cultural displacement.*

VIRTUAL SESSIONS
16 June 2025, Monday
09:00 – 10:30

12A   Work, Employment and Society V1

Join via MS Teams

Moderator: Saniye Dedeoğlu, Muğla University, Türkiye

2011   Losing Out or Gaining In? A Study on the Migratory Trends and the Propensity of Return of Healthcare Professionals from Turkey to Germany
Saniye Dedeoğlu, Çisel Ekiz Gökmen, Aslı Şahankaya Adar, Recep Kapar, Muğla University, Türkiye

953   Labour Out-Migration in Odisha: Processes, Determinants and Outcomes
Budhadev Mahanta, Jawaharlal Nehru University, New Delhi, India

785   Stay or Return: The Drivers of Mobility of East Asian Highly Skilled Immigrants in Mexico
Yu Huang, Nagoya University, Japan

570   Changes in Chinese Entrepreneurs' Perspectives on Business in Russia at the Turn of the 20th and 21st Centuries
Olga Zalesskaia, Blagoveshchensk State Pedagogical University, Russian Federation

12B   Identities and Migration V1

Join via MS Teams

Moderator: Lan Lo, University of Nottingham, UK

784   A Study of Russian Immigrants in Japan: Awareness and Sense of Belonging within Ethnic Communities
Khimchuk Svetlana, University of Tsukuba, Japan

673   Seeking Truth Across the Mediterranean Waves: Upholding the Rights of Families of Deceased Migrants
Charlotte Imhof, Institute of Legal Support and Technical Assistance, Laos
Jyothis Mary, Hume Institute for Postgraduate Studies, Switzerland

827   Multilingual possibilities in a Japanese high school: exploring immigrant students' belonging through identity texts
Isabel Sáenz-Hernández, Pompeu Fabra University, Spain
Sayaka Shima, University of Tsukuba, Japan
Wang Ziang, University of Tsukuba, Japan

451   Mother tongue and language learning motivation: a survey among
       Chinese immigrants living in Hungary
           Szandra Ésik, Eötvös Loránd University, Hungary
985   Gender-Based Challenges, Social Behavior, and Coping Mechanisms
       of Urban Migration in Pakistan
           Muhammad Atif, University of Agriculture Faisalabad, Pakistan

12C   Environment and Migration V1
Join via MS Teams
Moderator: Alfonso Sánchez Carrasco, Universidad Loyola Andalucía, Spain
515   Exploring the Climate Anxiety and Migration Nexus: Evidence from
       Copán, Honduras
           Alfonso Sánchez Carrasco, Universidad Loyola Andalucía, Spain
           Yolanda Hernández-Albújar, Universidad Loyola Andalucía, Spain
           Sergio Fernández-Artamendi, Universidad de Sevilla, Spain
706   To Stay Afloat: Examining the Nationality and Human Security Nexus
       of Climate-Induced Migrants from Sinking States
           *Emmanuel Chukwunweike Monyei, Ruhr University Bochum,
           Germany*
818   Shaping vulnerability in resettlement refugees integration processes
           Luzia Jurt, FHNW, Switzerland
           Sophie Suter, FHNW, Switzerland
966   Climate Migration and Policy Mismatch: Tensions between National
       and Supranational Actors
           Melek Özlem Ayas, İstanbul Beykent Üniversitesi, Türkiye

12D   Migration and Insecurity
Join via MS Teams
Moderator: K. Onur Unutulmaz, Ankara Social Sciences University, Türkiye
800   Impact of Experiences of War and Displacement on Collective
       Memory in Cyprus: Preliminary Results
           *Burcu Kaya Kızılöz, Shenel Husnu Raman, Aysenur Talat Zrilli,
           Eastern Mediterranean University, Cyprus*
986   Latin American Migration to Türkiye: Motivations, Experiences,
       Prospects
           Elif Sena Garrido Forner, Ankara Social Sciences University, Turkiye
679   Political Dissent and Migration: The Montenegrin Experience in
       Communist Yugoslavia
           *Jelisaveta Blagojević, Historical Institute of the University of
           Montenegro, Montenegro*

861   Migrant communities and heritage: towards a deterritorialization of culture
        Elena Carletti, University of Bari "Aldo Moro", Italy

16 June 2025, Monday
11:00 – 12:30
13A   Work, Employment and Society V2
Join via MS Teams

Moderator: Ruchi Singh, Tata Institute of Social Sciences. Mumbai Maharashtra, India

744   'Business is in the Blood': Migrant Entrepreneurship among Bangladeshi Men in England
        Shirley Andrea Velasquez-Hoque, Oxford Brookes University, England

716   Employability narratives in digital storytelling: do overqualified Brazilian and Venezuelan immigrants in Portugal tell the same story?
        Paulo Sousa Nascimento, University of Madeira, Portugal
        Magda Sofia Roberto, University of Lisbon, Portugal

2041   The Migration of Software Developers in The Context of the Hegemonic Influence of Relational Networks: A Mixed-Methods Study
        Şevket Burak Işık, Anadolu University, Türkiye
        Fuat Güllüpınar, Anadolu University, Türkiye

846   Employment of the Ukrainian Refugees in Latvia
        Gunta Pastore, University of Latvia, Latvia

13B   Identities and Migration V2
Join via MS Teams

Moderator: Mehmet Gökay Özerim, Yasar University, Türkiye

407   From 'creative class' to 'creative migrants': narratives of Turkish academics and artists navigating precarious employment, identities, and social positionings in the Nordics
        Nilay Kilinc, University of Helsinki, Finland

777   Beyond victimhood: The role of children's agency in shaping their educational outcomes in Romanian transnational families
        Georgiana Udrea, National University of Political Studies and Public Administration, Romania
        Oana-Gabriela Niculescu, National University of Political Studies and Public Administration, Romania

906   Online Anti-Immigration Sentiments: Emotional Drivers and
      Manipulative Strategies
      Mehmet Gökay Özerim, Yasar University, Türkiye
594   Security, Old Age and Irregular/Illegal Migration at Croatia's Eastern
      Borders
      *Sandra Cvikić, Institute of Social Sciences Ivo Pilar, Regioinal
      Center Vukovar, Croatia*
      Dražen Živić, Institute of Social Sciences Ivo Pilar, Zagreb, Croatia

13C   Law, Policy and Governance V1
Join via MS Teams
Moderator: Stefani Stojchevska, South East European University, Macedonia
823   The Role of the Hick-Hyman Law on Human-Computer Interaction
      (HCI) Systems in Extraterrestrial Migration: Contemporary
      Perspectives and Challenges
      Stefani Stojchevska, South East European University, Macedonia
642   The Right to Work of Foreign Nationals as a Starting Point for Proper
      Legal Integration
      Aitana Torró Calabuig, Universidad de Valencia, Spain
592   Marginalization as Resistance: Indonesian Migrant Domestic Workers
      and Grassroots Solidarity in Hong Kong's Governance Landscape
      Yiqiu Huang, University of Hong Kong, Hong Kong
932   Examining the Role of Dublin Regulations in the Securitization of EU
      Migration Policies and the Influence of the Far-Right
      Zeynep Naz Oral, University of Genoa, Italy

13D   Remittances and Development V1
Join via MS Teams
Moderator: Ibrahim Sirkeci, International Business School, Manchester, UK
786   Impact of Remittances on Socio-Economic Wellbeing of Gulf Migrants
      Family: A Study on Dalit Women Domestic Workers from Andhra
      Pradesh to Gulf Countries
      *Mekala Sagar, Centre for Economic and Social Studies, Hyderabad,
      India*
      *Y. Sreenivasulu, Centre for Economic and Social Studies,
      Hyderabad, India*
872   Climate Change, Macroeconomic Sensitivity and the Response of
      Remittances to Morocco: An Econometric Analysis
      Hajar Boudri, Mohammed V Rabat University, Morocco
      Boutaina Ismaili Idrissi, Mohammed V Rabat University, Morocco

684   Effect of Remittances on Poverty in the Western Balkan Countries
       Nevila Mehmetaj, University of Shkodra, Albania
858   The Impact of Official Development Aid and Remittances on
       Economic Growth: A Systematic Review by Prisma Method
       Boutaina Ismaili Idrissi, University Mohammed V Rabat, Morocco
       Ghita Zemmouri, University Mohammed V Rabat, Morocco

16 June 2025, Monday
13:30 – 15:00
14A   Education and Skilled Migration V1
Join via MS Teams

*Moderator: Mohammed Abdullahi, Coventry University, United
Kingdom*

766   Algorithmic Precarity: How AI Systems and PGWP Reform Reshape
       Canada's Educational Migration Pathways
       Andrea Lachmansingh, York University, Canada
       Sanjana Rahman, York University, Canada
       Aron Roman, York University, Canada
551   Forced migration and getting cohesion of Syrian children
       Vildan Mahmutoğlu, Galatasaray Üniversitesi, Türkiye
714   Bridging Policy and Practice: Inclusion of Refugee and Asylum-
       Seeking Children in Latvian Schools
       Zane Melke, University of Latvia, Latvia
925   The Dual Impacts of International Medical Migration:
       Nigerian Doctors in the UK and the Consequences for
       Nigeria's Healthcare System
       Mohammed Abdullahi, Coventry University, United Kingdom

14B   Türkiye ve Göç
Join via MS Teams

Moderator: Zeynep Banu Dalaman, Bahçeşehir University, Türkiye

983   Suriyeli Kadınların Barış Sürecine Yönelik Algıları ve Geri Dönüş
       Beklentileri: Nitel Bir Araştırma
       Zeynep Banu Dalaman, Bahçeşehir University, Türkiye
974   Anarşalı Selanik Göçmenlerinin Kültürel Bellek Bağlamında Mübadil
       Kimliklerinin Oluşumu
       Cansu Bitirim Kacar, Istanbul University, Türkiye
982   Göç, Aidiyet ve Kimlik: Türkiye'den İtalya'ya Göç Eden Ailelerin
       Çocuklarının Anavatan Kavramına Bakışı

Gül Ince-Beqo, Milan Üniversitesi, İtalya

14C   Insecurity and Migration

Join via MS Teams

Moderator: Ruth Elizabeth Prado Pérez, ITESO, Jesuit University of Guadalajara, Mexico

761   Bureaucratic Violence against Migrants and Refugees in Mexico
        Ruth Elizabeth Prado Pérez, ITESO, Jesuit University of Guadalajara, Mexico

569   Psychocultural Marginality and the Impact on Scottish Emigrants
        Janet Elizabeth Fetzer, Regent University, Virginia, USA
        Kara Woodley, University of Wisconsin-Superior, USA

908   Social movements in Ecuador and LGBTQI+ Venezuelan migration
        Juan Carlos Valarezo Sánchez, Pontificia Universidad Católica del Ecuador, Ecuador

676   The Rise of New Authoritarianism, Neoliberal Economics, and Mass Migration
        Anas Karzai, Laurentian University, Canada

14D   Theory, Data and Methods V1

Join via MS Teams

Moderator: Clemente Quinones-Reyes, Georgia Gwinnett College, USA

659   Impact of Aspirations and Capabilities to Migrate on Central American Migration to the USA
        Clemente Quinones-Reyes, Georgia Gwinnett College, USA

753   Refugee research ethics: moving from participation to mattering
        Maria Psoinos, Canterbury Christ Church University, UK

819   Intersectionality and Climate Migration: Understanding Vulnerabilities and Social Justice
        Betul Dilara Seker, Yuzuncu Yil University, Türkiye

978   Nigeria and Contemporary Issues of international Migration: A Critical Examination of Lee's Push-Pull Theory
        Mafos Steve, Peoples' Friendship University of Russia, Russian Federation

55

15A   Work, Employment and Society V3

Join via MS Teams

Moderator: Oshin Pandey, Hampshire College, USA

951   Migration flows and foreign direct investment: An Econometric
         Analysis
         Oumaima Bouarfa, University Sidi Mohamed Ben Abdellah,
         Morocco
         Mohammed Abdellaoui, University Sidi Mohamed Ben Abdellah,
         Morocco
         Hind Chamchoune, University Sidi Mohamed Ben Abdellah,
         Morocco
         Hajar El Bouch, University Sidi Mohamed Ben Abdellah, Morocco

767   Comparative Pathways of Transnational Labor Migration:
         Intermediaries and Political Economy in Nepal and Pakistan
         Oshin Pandey, Hampshire College, USA

763   Co-Production of Migrant Precarity by Sending and Receiving States:
         Bangladeshi Workers in the Gulf Region
         Sanjana P. Rahman, York University, Canada

696   From Migration to Reintegration: A Review of Social, Economic, and
         Psychological Challenges in Return Migration of Pakistani Students
         Waqas Ahmad, Huazhong University of Science and Technology,
         Wuhan, China

15B   Special Session: Research and Policy at the Intersection of
Migration Flows in Central America

Join via MS Teams

Moderator: Tom Hare, University of Notre Dame, USA

2014   Research and Policy at the Intersection of Migration Flows in Central
         America: Where Do We Go from Here?
         Tom Hare, University of Notre Dame, USA

2015   What Central American Youth's Future Ideation Tells Us about Their
         Migration Intentions
         María Estela Rivero Fuentes, University of Notre Dame, USA

2016   Measuring perceptions of hope and migration intentions in El
         Salvador: Lessons from the Hope Index
         Margarita Beneke de Sanfeliu, Fundación Salvadoreña para el
         Desarrollo Económico y Social, El Salvador

2017   International migration in Central America and the Dominican Republic: flows, dynamics and public policy responses
Alberto Mora Román, Estado de la Región, Costa Rica

2018   Governance of migration cycles in Mexico and Central America: Comparative analysis of institutional designs for the management of migration policies
Eduardo Nuñez, National Democratic Institute, Guatemala

15C   Identities and Migration V3

Join via MS Teams

Moderator: Suzy Ismail, Cornerstone Marriage & Family Intervention, USA

695   Unprocedural Removal of Protection Seekers, Legal Barriers and Changing Paradigm in Involuntary Migration: UK and US
Carol Ijeoma Njoku, University of San Francisco, USA

514   A Migration Model on Migrants with Undetermined Destination: The Journey of Chinese Diasporas in South America
Sing Ip Daniel Lai, McMaster Divinity College, Canada

771   Collectivism and Uncertainty Avoidance in Narrative Oral Histories of Resettled Syrian Refugees
Suzy Ismail, Cornerstone Marriage & Family Intervention, USA

599   Cosmologies of destination for tracing the roots and routes of young migrants
Irasema Mora-Pablo, University of Guanajuato, Mexico

15D   Retos de la migración siglo XXI – V1

Join via MS Teams

Moderator: Pascual García Macías, UTPL, Ecuador

747   Dimensiones del Bienestar en la Migración en Tránsito: Un Estudio Etnográfico de Migrantes Centroamericanos en Zacatecas, México
Pascual Gerardo García Zamora, Universidad Autónoma de Zacatecas, México
Aguilar Delgado Sayra Alejandra, México
Ruiz de Chávez Rámirez Dellanira, Universidad Autónoma de Zacatecas, México
Herrera Maartínez Juan Lamberto, Universidad Autónoma de Zacatecas, México

848   La frontera humanitaria de Tumbes (Perú): políticas migratorias y respuestas locales en el contexto del desplazamiento masivo y forzado venezolano (2018-2023)
Valentina Cappelletti, Pontificia Universidad Católica del Perú,

Perú
Valeria Aron Said, Georgetown University, USA

770 Vivir en las sombras: la migración latinoamericana en la Costa Sur del Golfo en los Estados Unidos
Nayeli Burgueño Angulo, Universidad Autónoma de Sinaloa, México
José Salvador Cueto Calderón, Universidad Autónoma de Sinaloa, México

16 June 2025, Monday
17:30 – 19:00
16A   Education and Skilled Migration V2

Join via MS Teams
Moderator: Lan Lo, University of Nottingham, UK

641 Bridging the Gap to Enhance Integration: Recognition of Low- and Medium-Skilled Migrant Workers' Qualifications
Aitana Torró Calabuig, Universidad de Valencia, Spain

666 Trans-Saharan Pathways and Transit Experiences among Sub-Saharan Migrants: A qualitative systematic review
Mawutor Fleku, University of Ghana, Ghana
Sarah Kwakye, University of Ghana, Ghana

807 Belonging Through Place: Student Migrants' Urban Narratives in Ankara
Oluwaseyi Igbekele Adeleye, Middle East Technical University, Turkey
Osman Balaban, Middle East Technical University, Turkey

812 Migrant caregivers and the experiences of the people around them in the nursing care workplace in Okayama, Japan: the voices from the migrant caregiver trainers
Etsuko Sakairi, Hashimoto Foundation Societas Research Institute, Japan

16B   Communication, Media, Culture and Migration

Join via MS Teams
Moderator: Patricia Posch, Communication and Society Research Centre (CECS), Portugal

890 Migrant Activism and Digital Black Feminism in Portugal's Media Landscape: The Case of Afrolis
Patricia Posch, Communication and Society Research Centre

(CECS), Portugal

740   This is why we stay: culture, identity and migration for the urban Zoques in Tuxtla Gutierrez, Chiapas, and the Raramuri in Ciudad Juarez, Chih
Andres F. Hijar, Georgia Gwinnett College, USA

2024   Virtual bonds across borders. Stay-behind children's perspectives on digital communication and transnational family relationships
Georgiana Udrea, National University of Political Studies and Public Administration, Romania
Gabriela Guiu, National University of Political Studies and Public Administration, Romania

987   Contrasting Ways of Representing Syrians in Türkiye: Mainstream vs. New Media Divide
K. Onur Unutulmaz, Ankara Social Sciences University, Türkiye

677   The Manufacture of Fear and the Politics of Cultural Fascism
Anas Karzai, Laurentian University, Canada

16C   Retos de la migración siglo XXI – V2

Join via MS Teams

Moderator: Pascual García Macías, UTPL, Ecuador

935   Desafíos socioeconómicos de la emigración italiana a México: una perspectiva histórica
Sara D'Anna Pompeu Fabra University, Spain

757   Narrativas sobre masculinidad y vulnerabilidad en la experiencia de varones migrantes
Diana Tamara Martínez Ruíz, Universidad Nacional Autónoma de México
Francisco Hernández Galván, Universidad Autónoma de Puebla, México
Alejandra Ceja Fernandez, ENES Morelia, UNAM, México

972   Migración italiana a México: Una perspectiva histórica
Sara D'Anna, Pompeu Fabra University, Spain

778   La migración indocumentada de niñas, niños y adolescentes sin acompañamiento en tránsito por México: retos y desafíos para la política migratoria Mexicana
Laura Natalia Rodríguez Ariano, Universidad Autónoma Metropolitana, México

Join via MS Teams

Moderator: Erin Lopez, Coalition for Humane Immigrant Rights (CHIRLA), USA

979   Climate Migration: The Next Era of Immigration
   Netta Avineri, PhD, The Middlebury Institute of International Studies at Monterey, USA
   Vladimir Carrasco, CHIRLA, USA
   Kevin Heller, The Middlebury Institute of International Studies at Monterey, USA
   Erin Lawrence, The Middlebury Institute of International Studies at Monterey, USA
   Erin Lopez, CHIRLA, USA
   Paulina Moreno, Community Action Board of Santa Cruz County, Inc., USA

980   CHIRLA Wildfire Relief 2025: Examining the Impact of the Palisades and Eaton Wildfires on Los Angeles' Immigrant Community
   Erin Lopez, CHIRLA, USA
   Tanairy Guzman Reyes, CHIRLA, USA

981   Understanding Reasons for Migration: Tapachula Field Survey
   Erin Lopez, CHIRLA, USA

17 June 2025, Tuesday
09:00 – 10:30
17A   Law, Policy and Governance V2

Join via MS Teams

Moderator: Edina Lilla Meszaros, University of Oradea, Romania

459   Refugees in neutral Portugal during the Second World War: hospitality and intransigence
   Carolina Henriques Pereira, University of Coimbra, Portugal

728   Has Romania the potential of becoming a country of destination for third-country nationals?
   Edina Lilla Meszaros, University of Oradea, Romania

593   Migration Processes in the Russian Far East: Yesterday, Today, and Tomorrow
   Evgenii Gamerman, Institute for Comprehensive Analysis of Regional Problems of the Far Eastern Branch of the Russian Academy of Sciences, Russia

573   Experiences of Iranian Global Talent Independent Visa Holders in Australia

Samantha Saidi, James Cook University (Townsville), Australia

17B   Space, Place and Migration V1
Join via MS Teams
Moderator: Alin Croitoru, Lucian Blaga University of Sibiu, Romania

840   Exploring Trends and Processes of Indian Labour Migration to Gulf Countries: A Case Study of Murshidabad District
   Abbasuddin Sk, North-Eastern Hill University, India
   Subrata Purkayastha, North-Eastern Hill University, India

525   Liquid Spatiotemporality: From Nomadic to Sedentary to Nomadic
   Bilal Salaam, İstanbul Ticaret University/İbn Haldun University, Türkiye

637   Refugee return from neighboring host countries in the developing world
   Md. Matiul Hoque Masud, Bangladesh

558   Exploring Romanians' Emigration Intentions Amid Recent Overlapping Crises
   Alin Croitoru, Lucian Blaga University of Sibiu, Romania

17C   Integration and Migration V1
Join via MS Teams
Moderator: Sadaf Mahmood, University of Agriculture, Faisalabad, Pakistan

786   Impact of Remittances on Socio-Economic Wellbeing of Gulf Migrants Family: A Study on Dalit Women Domestic Workers from Andhra Pradesh to Gulf Countries
   Mekala Sagar, Centre for Economic and Social Studies, Hyderabad, India
   Y. Sreenivasulu, Centre for Economic and Social Studies, Hyderabad, India

729   Multi-Generational Economic Assimilation: A Dynamic Convergence Analysis of Native and Immigrant Earnings in the UK, 2001-2023
   Rukhsana Kausar, University of Westminster, UK
   Issam Malki, University of Westminster, UK

665   Academic Integration Challenges and Psychological Well-being of International Students: A Study in China
   Rabia Mahmood, Huazhong University of Science and Technology, Wuhan, China
   Freda Yangrong Wang, Huazhong University of Science and Technology, Wuhan, China
   Sadaf Mahmood, University of Agriculture, Faisalabad, Pakistan

Waqas Ahmad, Huazhong University of Science and Technology, Wuhan, China

Rao Muhammad Faisal Suleman, Pakistan

984   Climate Change, Working Conditions, and Labor Migration: A Case Study of Pakistan

Sadaf Mahmood, University of Agriculture, Faisalabad, Pakistan

Rabia Mahmood, Huazhong University of Science and Technology, Wuhan, China

Uzma Niaz, Emerson University, Multan, Pakistan

Unsa Mahmood, Emerson University, Multan, Pakistan

17D   Türkiye ve Göç

Join via MS Teams

Moderator: Hatice Yaprak Civelek, Anadolu University, Türkiye

578   Mendilim Benek Benek, Ortası Çarkıfelek: 1989 Yılında Bulgaristan'dan Anadolu Bozkırına Gelen Küçük Kadınlarda Zorunlu Göçün Hafızası

Hatice Yaprak Civelek, Anadolu University, Türkiye

Gökhan Deniz Dinçer, Anadolu University, Türkiye

Kazım Demirer, Anadolu University, Türkiye

2042   İranlı Mülteci Kadınların Kimlik Arama Sürecinde Din Değiştirmeleri: Eskişehir'de Bir Saha Araştırması

Rayehe Mozafarian, Anadolu University, Türkiye

Fuat Güllüpınar, Anadolu University, Türkiye

2040   Akışkan Sınırların Güvenliğini Sağlama: Türkiye-İran Sınırında Göç Yönetimindeki Zorluklar ve Fırsatlar

Güven Şeker, Carleton University, Canada

17 June 2025, Tuesday

11:00 – 12:30

18A   Space, Place and Migration V2

Join via MS Teams

Moderator: Ruchi Singh, Tata Institute of Social Sciences. Mumbai Maharashtra, India

2038   From Coastal Erosion to Urban Struggles: The Impact of Climate Change on Migration

Ruchi Singh, Tata Institute of Social Sciences. Mumbai Maharashtra, India

Sambit Tripathy, Tata Institute of Social Sciences. Mumbai

Maharashtra, India

829   From Residents to 'New Citizens': Aspirations, Identities and Decision-Making of Internal Migrants in China
Shiyang Chen, University of Liverpool, UK/China

547   Religious refugees in the 21th century - The cases of Afghanistan and Syria
Alexia Kapsampeli, LSBF, Kapodistrian University, Greece

553   Physical and Social Reflections of Migration on the City of Istanbul
Ayşe Nilay Evcil, İstanbul Beykent University, Türkiye
Şen Yüksel, İstanbul Beykent University, Türkiye

18B   Gender and Migration V2

Join via MS Teams

Moderator: Loshana Sivanarul, University College London, UK

963   Addressing the High Prevalence of Gestational Diabetes Mellitus (GDM) Among South Asian Immigrant Women in Canada: Causes, Consequences, and Potential Interventions
Loshana Sivanarul, UCL, UK

415   Femintegra – The labour trajectories of Romanian immigrant women in Barcelona, Valencia and Castellon
Ioana-Felicia Marin, University of Valencia, Spain

504   Socio-political conflicts and migration routes of Rwandan women in Cameroon
Signe Made Carelle Michèle, University of Yaoundé 1, Cameroon

583   An Intersectional Approach to the Study of the Integration of Sub-Saharan Migrant Women in Souss Massa
Siham Soulaimi, Ibn Zohr University, Morocco

18C   Retos de la migración siglo XXI - V2

Join via MS Teams

Moderator: Pascual García Macías, UTPL, Ecuador

656   El Chat la Para Ayuda Migratoria en México
Francisco José D´Angelo Ohep, México

2023   El Régimen de Deportación Fronterizo y la (Im)posibilidad de sus Fugas
María José Morales Vargas, Universidad Autónoma de Tlaxcala, México

612   El éxodo migratorio ecuatoriano en el primer cuarto del siglo XXI
Pascual García Macías, UTPL, Ecuador
Ruben García Zamora, Universidad Autonoma de Zacatecas,

México

579   The Accessibility of Migrants to Utilize Equine-Assisted Therapy for Trauma Treatment Associated with PTSD
> *Caroline Anna Erviksaeter, Western Norway University of Applied Sciences, Norway*

975   Social integration of immigrants and refugees through intersectionality and advantageousness: implications from the case study of Sancaktepe neighborhood
> *Isil Zeynep Turkan Ipek, Yeditepe University, Türkiye*
> *Gökçe Bayındır Goularas, Yeditepe University, Türkiye*
> *Yunus Mecit Öztürk, Yeditepe University, Türkiye*

18D   Migration and Integration

Join via MS Teams

Moderator: Isil Zeynep Turkan Ipek, Yeditepe University, Türkiye

579   The Accessibility of Migrants to Utilize Equine-Assisted Therapy for Trauma Treatment Associated with PTSD
> *Caroline Anna Erviksaeter, Western Norway University of Applied Sciences, Norway*

975   Social integration of immigrants and refugees through intersectionality and advantageousness: implications from the case study of Sancaktepe neighborhood
> *Isil Zeynep Turkan Ipek, Yeditepe University, Türkiye*
> *Gökçe Bayındır Goularas, Yeditepe University, Türkiye*
> *Yunus Mecit Öztürk, Yeditepe University, Türkiye*

455   Pre-migration capital, refugee journeys, and post-migration trajectories: a sequence analysis approach
> *Lidwina Gundacker, Institute for Employment Research (IAB) and University of Bamberg, Germany*

875   Unaccompanied minors and the Morie fires aftermath – A case study
> *Maria Dimou, International Hellenic University, Greece*
> *Stavros Marko, International Hellenic University, Greece*
> *Reggina Mantanika, International Hellenic University, Greee*

17 June 2025, Tuesday
13:30 – 15:00
19A   Identity and Wellbeing

Join via MS Teams

Moderator: Fatemeh Bakhshalizadeh, Iowa State University, USA

447   "I'm Now Like a Single Mother": Navigating Gendered Identity as a Dependent Spouse in the U.S.

Anastasia Ngozi Iwuagwu, University of South Florida, USA

479   Navigating family separation during displacement: experiences of refugee men in the UK

Dafni Katsampa, University of Hertfordshire, UK

873   Beyond Homogeneity: Understanding South Asian Cultural Diversity in the Canadian Context

Monisha Poojary, York University, Canada

541   Resilience and Professional Identity among F-2 Visa Spouses in the United States: Coping with Career Constraints under Immigration Policies

Fatemeh Bakhshalizadeh, Iowa State University, Ames, Iowa, USA

19B   Integration and Migration V2

Join via MS Teams

Moderator: Rashin Lamouchi, University of Victoria, Canada

550   Sense of belonging as 'being at home': Narratives of forced migrant youth in Southeast Asia

Rashin Lamouchi, University of Victoria, Canada

Leah Brathwaite, University of Toronto, Canada

820   Acculturation of Unaccompanied Children in Turkey: Challenges and Policy Implications

Betul Dilara Seker, Yuzuncu Yil University, Türkiye

401   Inherited welcoming practices? How previous migratory experiences shape newcomers' reception in rural Spain

Leticia Santaballa Santos, Societies in Motion Research Team (ESOMI) – Universidade da Coruña & CISPAC, Spain

Laura Oso Casas, Societies in Motion Research Team (ESOMI) – Universidade da Coruña & CISPAC, Spain

457   Home Literacy Environment of Rural-Urban Migrant Children with Different Length of Residence: Characteristics and the Association with SES and Parental Expectation

Yuchen Song, Xi'an Jiaotong Liverpool University, China

19C   Migración e identidad

Join via MS Teams

Moderator: Luz Elena Arozqueta, Universidad Iberoamericana, México

880   Solastalgia y migración. Reflexiones ante la pérdida y el desarraigo

Luz Elena Arozqueta, Universidad Iberoamericana, México

540   Migración e identidad : del odio a la integración en Trayectoria de la

bala de Luis Araújo

Ouadi-Chouchane Ibtissam, Strasbourg University, France

533   Racismo e inmigración: dos realidades entrelazadas
M. Isabel Garrido Gómez, Universidad de Alcalá, España

561   Desafíos en la salud de los migrantes mexicanos en situación irregular
en los Ángeles, California.
Nubia Alejandrina García Bárcenas, Pascual García Macías,
Dellanira Ruiz de Chávez Ramírez
Universidad Autónoma de Zacatecas, México

19D   Law, Policy and Governance V3

Join via MS Teams

Moderator: Lauren Herckis, CGFNS International, Inc. and Carnegie Mellon University, USA

653   Recent trends in transnational nurse migration: A regulatory
perspective
Lauren Herckis, CGFNS International, Inc. and Carnegie Mellon
University, USA

638   Bridging Fragmentation in the Regulation of Economic Migration
Christian Benedikt Offermanns, University of Sydney and
Thammasat University, Germany

2010   Governing the Migration of Turkish Health Professionals: Pushing
Forward or Pulling Back?
Saniye Dedeoğlu, Muğla University, Türkiye
Aslı Şahankaya Adar, Muğla University, Türkiye
Çisel Ekiz Gökmen, Muğla University, Türkiye
Recep Kapar, Muğla University, Türkiye

903   The Political Economy of Haitian Migration (2010–2025): U.S Foreign
Policy, Governance, Corruption, and Instability
Emmanuela Douyon, Columbia University, USA

423   An Analysis of Nigeria's Migration Policies and Their Compliance with
International Human Rights Standards
Tobiloba Awotoyr, Lead City University, Nigeria

Presenters Name Index

www.ingramcontent.com/pod-product-compliance
Lightning Source LLC
Chambersburg PA
CBHW060518280326
41933CB00014B/3019

9781801353281